THE
HOLY
SPIRIT

MALCOLM BURTON

Dedication

I celebrate the work of God.

l celebrate His workers in the U.S.

I celebrate His workers laboring abroad.

Forever thanks to my Aunt, the Rev. Mrs Norine Blum. It was under her teaching ministry in the Plum Grove, Texas Assembly of God Children's Church that the Word of God came alive to me.

As Aunt Norine spoke I realized she was not describing "television shows". She was speaking of real people. The Holy Spirit used her to bring revelation knowledge of the Word of God into my life. That deposit of the Holy Spirit is still alive and active today. Aunt Norine and my Uncle Harold pastored a successful church in a tough place for many years. I honor them.

Evangelist Jeff Taylor of Atlanta, Georgia is my younger brother in the Lord, and often partners with me in presenting in The School of the Holy Spirit. Pastor Lon McVeigh and I have been in relationship for almost 40 years and he continued to believe in me when others stopped. These two have teamed to make a very profound difference in my life. I celebrate each of you and the difference you are making in His Kingdom.

And deep, heartfelt thanks to Dr. David Yanez of RevMedia Publishing for helping my dreams become reality.

Why I Wrote This Book

We were "out back" that hot, humid day.

Granny Blum had a wraparound screened porch. We were on the North side facing the creek that ran into the East Fork of the San Jacinto River. Granny fanned herself as she and Mom talked of revival in our home church in rural Plum Grove, Texas.

They spoke animatedly of different people coming to Christ. Some were described as "hard cases."

Fascinated, I asked, "When will I be old enough to be saved?"

"If you've got gumption enough to ask, you can be saved now," Granny replied.

Mama had me repeat the Believer's Prayer. In the best traditions of Pentecostalism, the pair then rejoiced loudly over my salvation experience. Years passed by. One Sunday, I shared the story of that day with my congregation. Afterward a lady said, "Aren't you glad your grandmother told you about Jesus?"

In that precious moment, the light of understanding flooded me: If the Holy Spirit hadn't revealed Jesus to Granny, she would have had nothing to share with me.

My quest during the past 30 years of ministry has been knowing the Holy Spirit. He is a person Who loves conversation, but will force Himself on no one.

He is a revealer.

I am thankful He revealed Jesus to me. I am so appreciative He reveals the Word to me. Above all, I'm thankful He reveals Himself to us. *"In His presence is fullness of joy..."* (Psalm 16:11).

Pursing Him in His presence...

Malcolm Burton
Madison County, TX
June 2016

Table of Contents

Chapter One

The Multi-Faceted Works of the Holy Spirit

The Holy Spirit is a Creator.

He creates through His gifts and person.

He destroys the works of evil through believers.

He communicates more than anyone I have encountered.

The Holy Spirit Uses Men and Women to Reveal Hidden Things

Let me read something said about me by my spiritual father, the Rev. Dr. Ron Smith. This is an excerpt from the commendations section of my book *Miracles in Black and White*. Some of the statements, while greatly appreciated, are human observations. The insight from Dr. Smith is spiritual in nature. One of the big keys is it contains insight. "My spiritual son has the ability to communicate across social, financial and ethnic lines. The Holy Spirit enables him to reveal life-changing thoughts."

The Holy Spirit reveals hidden things that must be known on planet earth.

Some years ago I had the honor of helping the legendary Dr. Lester Sumrall write a book on this subject. Chief among the impressions of that time is the enhanced understanding I gained from hearing Dr. Sumrall tell stories from his life that illustrate the revelatory abilities of the Holy Spirit.

We need to know the Revealer.

King Nebuchadnezzar, a man who could only be described as wicked, was moved by the Holy Spirit acting in His role as revealer. *"The king answered Daniel, and said, "Truly your God is the God of gods, the Lord of kings, and a revealer of secrets, since you could reveal this secret,"* (Daniel 2:47)

When the gifts of the Holy Spirit are in manifestation, we have a promise that men and women will be moved to the place of repentance. This is because the Revealer is at work.

Ponder Paul's description of what happens when the Word of Knowledge is manifest. *"And thus the secrets of his heart are revealed; and so, falling down on his face, he will worship God and report that God is truly among you..."* (1 Corinthians 14:25).

Finis Dake, one of the great scholars of my time, wrote, "The chief end of all gifts and worship services is to bring men to repentance and surrender to God."

King David made a remarkable request of the Holy Spirit, *"Who can understand his errors? Cleanse me from secret sins. Keep back Your servant also from presumptuous sins; Let them not have dominion over me. Then I shall be blameless, And I shall be innocent of great transgression,"* (Psalms 19:12-13).

When I do not know what to do, I repent. In that moment I need Him to reveal hidden things because I do not want unconfessed sin or unknown heart attitudes to hinder the Holy Spirit's work through me.

Three Hidden Things the Revealer Handles

1. Some behavior patterns are so ingrained we are unaware of them.

2. Some behavior issues are so much a part of people that they do not really consider them wrong because they are unaware of them.

3. Some behavioral things are fully surfaced and the individual is aware of them but ashamed to deal with them.

The Holy Spirit facilitates our communication to God and brings His messages back to us. We can move forward in faith as hidden things are revealed and we choose to become more like Him.

One of my students will send me text messages during the day. If they begin with "A1", I know she is not referring to steak sauce. She is saying, "I want to be held accountable in this area." Some days she sends me a series of GPS maps indicating where she is. Why?

"A1."

Two days ago she sent an "A1" with a copy of her American Express statement. Why? She likes finer things but her highest priority is funding the Kingdom and coming out of debt. This American Express "A1" is because the Holy Spirit revealed a potential problem spot for her.

The Central Focus of This Book

We are living in the age of grace. Because of this God has made an amazing promise.

"And it shall come to pass in the last days, says God, That I will pour out of My Spirit on all flesh; Your sons and your daughters shall prophesy, Your young men shall see visions, Your old men shall dream dreams," ACTS 2:17

The focus of this book is: *The Holy Spirit will be poured out on us. We will receive His infilling and His gifts will begin to manifest through us.*

The gifts of the Holy Spirit did not come into manifestation for me during a time of incredible victory. They had always functioned in a limited manner. However, they came with a rush when I was in a crisis and cried out for an answer.

The church I served was "in reverse". I reached. He reached back. His gifts began to manifest and our church was never the same.

You may feel like your personal life is in reverse. It is not time to mourn or quit. It is time to reach!

When I reached, I found Him reaching back. When you reach you will find Him reaching back for you.

A Truth Inspired by a Natural Gift

Someone I love gave me a package of drinks I enjoy. They require mixing. This friend even put a blender in the pack. She said, "I do not give incomplete gifts." Her statement touched my heart, but more importantly, it spoke to my spirit.

Consider this verse again: *"And it shall come to pass in the last days, says God, that I will pour out of My Spirit on all flesh;"* (Acts 2:17A). If the gifts of the Holy Spirit were not for us today, I believe there would be no desire within the heart of the believer to receive them. If spiritual gifts were only for the Pope, Bishops, Pastors, Superintendents and TV Preachers, why would you desire their manifestation in your life?

The words *"...All flesh..."* make a powerful point. This means the ability of God will work through anyone. Male, or female. Youth, or adult. Rich, or poor. Uneducated, or profoundly learned.

God *Does* Discriminate

Discriminate is an amazing word. We routinely hear it associated with prejudice. But it, in the most general manner means, "...to tell the difference."

God can "tell the difference" between those who seek Him by faith and those who do not.

Many people are walking around with no understanding of what is to come. While God does not enjoy this He will not reward the unfocused. He rewards those who desire to know and do His will.

The Revealer desires to unfold your future to you. "However when He, the Spirit of truth, has come He will guide you into all truth; for He will not speak on His own authority, but whatever He hears He will speak; and He will tell you things to come" (John 16:13).

What a majestic revelation of His own good nature. God desires to bring revelation truth to those who are in Him. *"As each one has received a gift, minister it to one another, as good stewards of the manifold grace of God,"* (1 Peter 4:10).

The Holy Spirit is not a cover-up man.

The Holy Spirit is a revealer.

The most powerful thing He desires to reveal is His own goodness so we can be *"...able ministers..."* (2 Corinthians 3:6).

We have the opportunity to be a life-giver, sharer and restorer.

Chapter Two

The Holy Spirit Today

We are in the midst of the greatest outpouring known to mankind. It is because of this I do not become discouraged by the events I see.

Since the early 1900's we have been in the age of what I will refer to as the Charismatic Outpouring. Some may find this statement to be extreme, but I believe this move of God we find ourselves in is even more impressive than the Protestant Reformation as the power of God is restored to the church.

During my lifetime nothing has excited the church and stirred more controversy than the Charismatic Renewal.

A Powerful Truth

"No group persecutes the current move of God more than the people used of God in the last move,"
–Dr. Edwin Louis Cole.

By its nature"The Organized Church" restricted the move of God. Hierarchy seems to expand to fill the space left by our lack of understanding of the move of God. Well-meaning men and women create programs to manage the move of God.

My solution: Let the Holy Spirit Flow!

We are in the fourth generation of the "modern" outpouring. I cannot visit a single Full-Gospel Church that is not populated with people who came into the move of the Holy Spirit from other segments of Christianity.

Where Did We Come From?

One of the greatest weaknesses of the fourth generation is their lack of knowledge of where we came from. We can always learn from the Bible. A lesson from history is contained in Exodus 1: 8: "Now there arose up a new king over Egypt, which knew not Joseph."

Hands Off

Religion by nature is restrictive. The Charismatic move was such a spontaneous activity of the Holy Spirit, formal religion had no chance to "bottle it up".

Unrestricted by religious trappings, the move of God spilled out across the United States and around the globe. One proof of the authenticity of this move is that it took place with little formal training for the leaders, but managed to be completely in line with New Testament teaching.

The News Media routinely describes Islam as the fastest growing religion on earth. This is untrue. Christianity is still the largest... *and the fastest growing.*

While much of traditional Christianity in the US is contracting, even dying, Charismatic Christianity is still expanding. People in denominational churches that are withdrawing from Biblical standards of morality are fueling the growth of Full-Gospel Churches. During the first half of the 20th Century the most despised segment of Christianity was the group described as "Pentecostal. Today people continue to flock to these type of churches. Of the 20 largest churches in the US, 17 are part of this movement.

Due to the abuses of some segments calling themselves "Pentecostal", I am more likely to refer to myself as Spirit-Filled or Charismatic. The bottom line is I am in favor of the well-governed but unrestricted move of the Holy Spirit of the Living God.

The Charismatic Era

The Charismatic Movement was birthed in the 1960's primarily from the receptivity to the actions of the Holy Spirit, among Catholics influenced by "Pentecostal Revival" with the priests of Notre Dame University. Episcopal Christians, led by Dennis and Rita Bennett, ignited another outburst of the fire of God's Spirit.

While millions of denominational believers left their traditional churches, and affiliated with Pentecostal churches, the vast majority did not. Over time they became affiliated with what are known today as "Independent Charismatic" congregations.

Bible Evidence

The Bible evidence of Spirit Baptism is tongues. When the believer is filled with the Holy Spirit he speaks in the"tongue of initial evidence." This has been the pattern since the birthday of the church. *"When the Day of Pentecost had fully come, they were all with one accord in one place. And suddenly there came a sound from heaven, as of a rushing mighty wind and it filled the whole house where they were sitting. Then there appeared to them divided tongues, as of fire, and one sat upon each of them. And they were all filled with the Holy Spirit and began to speak with other tongues, as the Spirit gave them utterance."* (Acts 2:1-4).

Tongues is a spiritual language that is not known to the speaker. The believer speaks as the Holy Spirit gives the ability to speak. We will share more on this subject in a later chapter.

My Surprising Experience with Brother Ernest

During my days at Splendora High School I met a remarkable man named Ernest Johnson. He was the pastor of the largest Southern Baptist Church in my area. This particular congregation is known to believe in "cessation".

They believe and teach that all supernatural activity, including miracles of healing and the manifestation gifts of the Holy Spirit, ceased at the time of the death of the last apostle.

Bother Ernest heard of a critical need in the High School as one of our English teachers resigned and the district was unable to secure a replacement. A proud graduate of Baylor University, Brother Johnson took on the task, with the agreement the class he taught was primarily engaged in writing assignments, based upon books we read and our follow-up classroom discussions. A regular part of our discussions somehow seemed to repeatedly return to Biblical themes.

One day we turned to the topic of miracles. Brother Johnson shocked his largely Baptist class by declaring, "I believe miracles are for today." Some of his church members in the room challenged him, "You can't believe that. You're a Baptist." Brother Johnson said something that amazed me. "Yes, I am a Baptist. But I'm a different kind of Baptist." Our private conversations revealed he had experienced the infilling of the Holy Spirit with the evidence of speaking with other tongues.

Ours was a mutually enriching experience. Later in life he often introduced me to his congregation by saying, "I was a seminary graduate working on my doctorate, but I met a high school boy who knew the Holy Spirit in a way I did not know Him." We remained friends and in close contact until he ascended to be with our Lord.

The Original Shock and Awe Campaign

During the second phase of the Gulf War the Bush Administration called the initiation of the 2003 retaliatory attacks "Shock and Awe." Yet I submit to you this was nothing in comparison to the "Shock and Awe" produced by the Charismatic Outpouring.

Jesus caused the Holy Spirit to show up in a remarkably unique way, manifesting Himself as the giver of what had been thought of as "Pentecostal Experiences," to the non-Pentecostal portion of Christianity.

Completely surprised as I was by Brother Ernest's testimony, I was completely bowled over by testimonies to come. I had a hard time believing it when the pastor of the United Methodist Church in the"high rent" district of our area became Spirit-Filled.

As a young man in ministry, I was shocked by an invitation to preach at what is now known as the Catholic Charismatic Renewal Center. In those days, it was simply a Catholic congregation. The pastor was a man who had received the Holy Spirit and heard of my success in preaching and ministering on this topic.

At the time it made perfect sense to my egotistical self that he would invite me. Now I can only describe it as the hand of the Lord. Our times together were remarkable and hundreds were filled with the Holy Spirit during the meetings. The priest would introduce me and I would preach on receiving the Holy Spirit. We would minister in the altars together.

That relationship was lost because I did not understand his strong ties to Catholicism. I pushed too hard in a couple of areas and eventually lost his friendship. This tragic outcome is something I strongly regret to this day.

The Church Was Redefined

So many of these people came from cultures where the church building was considered to be holy and the only place mankind could meet with God. After coming into a fuller understanding of salvation and the infilling of the Holy Spirit1 they were glad to meet anywhere other believers were gathering to honor His presence.

The Holy Place today is known to live in the heart.

Chapter Three

Charisma

Charisma means spiritual gift.

We routinely use the word charismatic.

We do not always use it in regard to spiritual things.

Very often we use it in defining someone's personality.

Yet, the proper connotation of charismatic personality is that it be used to gain and hold the attention of another until God's message can be shared.

Basis for the Supernatural

Charisma is the basis for the supernatural.

We are living in a world that is starved for miracles.

Charisma is a supernatural ability bestowed upon an individual through the infinite strength of God. All "Charismas" *(Charismata)* are bestowed upon believers for the purpose of serving the local church.

Two-Fold Function of Charisma

1. **The Release of Power.** "You shall receive power after he Holy Spirit is come upon you,'1 (Acts 1:8). You are not in this alone. Jesus went back to heaven but the Holy Spirit stayed.

2. **Destroying the Strategies of Hell.** *"I give you power over*

all the works of the evil one. And the strategy concocted at the gates of hell will not prevail against you," (Matthew 16:17-18). Strategy was concocted in a particular place. This strategy was to be arrayed against a particular people in a particular place.

Strategies have been drawn up against us for each stage of our life but they are often variations of the same theme. We are in the midst of the struggle of the ages. Satan obviously believes he can win by destroying the church. One of the most positive things we can do for the Kingdom is believe and state that it cannot be defeated.

We empower hell each time we describe Christianity as being in bad shape. Yes, there is a war on. We are seeing what appear to be losses. But this is not the end. The end will be different.

I Am Not Oblivious

Yes, I notice when attendance is not what it should be.

Yes, I notice when people who once couldn't stand to miss a service find it difficult to get back in the car for Wednesday night. But I am not willing to declare Christianity is in trouble because the Holy Spirit outpouring continues around the world. I did not find anyone among the believers in Singapore, China or South Korea who was ignorant of the move of the Holy Spirit. The only people who spoke against the outpouring were those from or trained in the United States.

America is in trouble, but we will win. Yes, I "see" the moral rot afflicting our nation in the name of tolerance. However, instead of only speaking the negative, I stir my faith with the prophecy of Evangelist Reinhardt Bohnke, "America will be saved. God will not forget the nation that did not forget the rest of the world."

I, Malcolm Burton, will not forget the rest of the world. I will not forget those in demonic bondage in Muslim lands. I will not forget those in demonic bondage in polytheistic lands. I will not forget the most "gospel hardened" nation on earth, what was formerly known as East Germany.

Qualify For the Work

Qualification is part of every interview process.

The interviewer decides if we are qualified to do the job.

We must be qualified spiritually in order to do the work of God on earth. That is why this book focuses on the person and gifts of the Holy Spirit.

The Holy Spirit is our *qualifier*. He makes sure we are equal to the task. He is our equalizer. He makes us more than equal to any task before us.

He is our *warfare expert*. King David wrote, "Blessed be the LORD my strength which teaches my hands to war, and my fingers to fight: (Psalm 144: 1). This Old Testament verse helps us see the gifts of the Holy Spirit even serve in teaching us how to use them to our benefit and the benefit of those around us.

As we qualify, two things happen:

1. We learn spiritual gifts exist.
2. We learn how to use them to benefit the Body of Christ and the lost.

Why Am I Here?

Dr. Winetta Flakes is a sister in the Lord. She told me something I said that revealed me to her. "I watched you walk through the parking lot and wondered how you would manage to make it through the service. Then you took the pulpit and looked as if nothing was going on with your body. I spoke to you about it and you said something that intrigued me: "I am only alive when I am doing the work of God. That is why I am still here."

That insight into me was one I had missed. But it also was an insight into Winetta. She wondered why she was so strange... because she feels most alive when she is preaching or praying for others.

It is why she is here. Read Ephesians 4:10-11:

> *"He who descended is also the One who ascended far above all the heavens, that He might fill all things. And He Himself gave some to be apostles, some prophets, some evangelists, and some pastors and teachers,"*

When do you feel most alive?

This is an insight to your gifting.

Can you tell me in a short sentence why you are here on earth?

"My goal is gain insight into the spirit realm and share that supernatural knowledge with believers who desire to go deeper into the things of God," –Malcolm Burton

Goals For My Students

1. Know what the Charismatic gifts are.

2. Be able to discuss spiritual gifts fluently and freely.

3. Know how to use spiritual gifts for their maximum benefit.

I have seen things other men did not see because I have stood on the shoulders of giants...men like Dr. Ron Smith. "Expect spiritual gifts to operate out in the marketplace where the people are. Instead of expecting demonic manifestations, anticipate opportunities for the power of God to be displayed,"

–Dr. Ron Smith, my spiritual father.

Jesus was a man empowered by the Holy Spirit. It was not the deity of Jesus that cast out the evil spirits from the man of Gadara. It was Jesus the man flowing in the gifts of the Holy Spirit. Read Luke 8:26-39.

Stir your expectation concerning spiritual gifts. If you have never been used in spiritual gifts, ask God to use you.

I pray that fear of failure or embarrassment will not keep you from allowing God use you in these powerful forces for change.

Faith Confession:

"I will ask God to use me in the gifts of His Holy Spirit each day. He will give me insight that will help me to live in victory so I can help those around me. I declare this in Jesus Name."

Chapter Four

Does the Supernatural Still Exist?

The supernatural is for today.

Yet many churches will not preach this.

They will speak about the work of the evil one.

They will even describe how satan is doing great (supernatural) evil. But they seem to lose sight of the fact God created Lucifer who became satan and is clearly superior to him.

> *"Then He called His twelve disciples together and gave them power and authority over all devils, and to cure diseases. And He sent them to preach the kingdom of God and to heal the sick,"* (Luke 9:1-2)

Each visitation of the Holy Spirit brings strength and demonstrations of power. Note what happened with Peter. He spoke from his spirit and 3000 people were saved in a great open-air meeting.

> *"Now when they heard this, they were cut to the heart, and said to Peter and the rest of the apostles, "Men **and** brethren what shall we do?" Then Peter said to them, "Repent and let every one of you be baptized in the name of Jesus Christ for the remission of sins; and you shall receive the gift of the Holy Spirit. For the promise is to you and to your children, and to all who are afar off as many as the Lord our God will call,"* (Acts 2:37-39)

What Peter did not become in three years of walking with Jesus He became in a single afternoon with the Holy Spirit. Peter boldly preached profound truth by revelation of the Holy Spirit we still benefit from today.

1. **Repent.** Declare you believe the witness of the Blood of Jesus applied to the Mercy Seat when He ascended back to heaven.

2. **Be Baptized.** Jesus was water baptized and we should be, too.

3. **Receive the Holy Spirit.** Allow God to produce the evidence you have been Spirit Baptized.

4. **Declare the Promise To Others.** Who is this promise to? It is to everyone who will receive. The Bible teaches, *"For whoever calls on the name of the LORD shall be saved,"* (Romans 10:13). The principle we use today is that the Name of Jesus opens the door into the Kingdom and into the deeper things of God.

Two Overlooked Truths

1. The outpouring on the Day of Pentecost came with the stated promise it was what God wanted to do. There is no record of God having changed either His thoughts or methodology.

2. This outpouring began with repentance. When I do not know what to do, I repent because I do not want unknown heart attitudes to block the blessings of God from my life. Since the call of God linked the outpouring to repentance, so long as repentance exists on the earth the command to receive the Holy Spirit will remain on the earth.

Who Is This Outpouring For?

God started something more than 2,000 years ago.

> *"And it shall come to pass afterward That I will pour out My Spirit on all flesh; Your sons and your daughters shall prophesy, your old men shall dream dreams, your young men shall see visions. And also on **My** menservants and on **My** maidservants I will pour out My Spirit in those days."* (Joel 2:28-29)

Men, women and children, the young, middle aged and old are all qualified to receive the Holy Spirit today.

Seven Fruits of This Blessing:

1. Love of the Word of God.

2. Understanding of the Need for Financial Prosperity.

3. A Culture of Quick Repentance from Sin.

4. Compassion-based Evangelism.

5. Highly Developed Ministries of Benevolence.

6. People of Praise and Worship.

7. Manifestations of Spiritual Healing.

Chapter Five

Foundations of Spiritual Gifts

There is indescribable unity the Trinity.

Their level of submission is so profound as to be indescribable.

Paul wrote 1 Corinthians as a single letter. While we will pay special attention to Chapters 12 and 14, it is wise to read the entire book in order to have fuller understanding of the truth Paul was sharing.

The Body of Christ is one complete structure. In order for it to function properly there cannot be the barriers brought about by egotistical individuals who believe their way is the only way. While some have more impressive behavior than others, no one is better than anyone else.

What am I saying? There must be unity.

Chapter 13 drives home another critically important point: Love is essential. Without love we cannot function as believers and spiritual gifts will not properly work for us. As we read Chapter 13 it is best to remember it is not separate from Chapter 12. It is just an amplification of Chapter 12.

Something I Believe God Desires

Television changed everything. The ease of access of the internet brought about even more change. It is now very easy for a sense of ministerial "self-promotion" to reign in the Lord's Body.

Dr. Lester Sumrall, in his book the Gifts and Ministries of the Holy

Spirit, said, "No one who is being used by the Holy Spirit is unique within himself; he is unique only in that he is permitted to be part of the Body."

To quote Granny Blum, "The Holy Spirit is not interested in 'Big I' and 'Little You.' He is only interested in how greatly you want to be used."

God's Plainly Stated Desire

"Now about the gifts of the Spirit, brothers and sisters, I do not want you to be uninformed," (1 Corinthians 12:1)

Could God possibly declare this more plainly? I think not. He does not want us to be walking in ignorance. He expects us to be knowledgeable about the function of His spiritual gifts.

Diverse Gifts

Within the nine gifts of the Holy Spirit are three categories: revelation, power and inspiration. "There are diversities of gifts, but the same Spirit. 5 there are differences of ministries, but the same Lord.6 And there are diversities of activities, but it is the same God who works all in all." (1 Corinthians 12:4-6). All three groups flow from the one Holy Spirit.

Diverse Administrations

Joel Osteen and I are both pastors. The last time I saw his annual budget for Lakewood Church it was $103 Million. The last year I was at Northgate, ours was about $200,000.

What is the difference? Same gift. Different dollar amounts? We ministered to different numbers of people. His administration was larger than mine. Read verse five again, *"There are differences of ministries, but the same Lord."* We can be called to the same office, be doing things differently and yet serve the same Lord. This is why we do not look up or down on anybody. We are all serving the same

Lord. He is the Lord who does the little things and the big things.

"God has always made me more," is a statement I made over lunch to a friend. She is a devout lady from a non-Charismatic background and someone I would characterize as hungry for more of God. She was profoundly touched by the thought.

God wants you to live a profitable life. One of His ways of bringing this to pass is through the Gifts of the Holy Spirit.

1 Corinthians 12:8-10 outlines the Charismatic Gifts: *"...for to one is given the word of wisdom through the Spirit, to another the word of knowledge through the same Spirit, to another faith by the same Spirit, to another gifts of healings by the same Spirit, to another the working of miracles, to another prophecy, to another discerning of spirits, to another different kinds of tongues, to another the interpretation of tongues."*

God Never Gives Up His Voice

Before studying there, let us focus for a few minutes on verse 11: *"But one and the same Spirit works all these things, distributing to each one individually as He wills."*

Consider the last three words of verse 11, "...as He wills." He has the final right to speak in every area of our life and we must give this right to Him in order to truly prosper.

He knows your capacity.

He knows what you can and cannot do.

Allow Him to give gifts to you as He desires.

He will not be limited...*if you will not limit Him.*

Diverse but Together

"For as the body (The Human Body) is one and has many members

(collectively), but all the members of that one body, being many, are one body, so also is Christ," (1 Corinthians 12:12 NKJV Insertions mine). The Body of Christ reflects the human body in that it has many parts. All these many parts come together to make a functioning whole.

Make Your Life A Schism Free Zone

We must have a clear understanding of the need for strife-free living in order for the gifts of the Holy Spirit to flow. It is my belief that strife is the single greatest pollutant to be found in the River of God. Not only does it displease our Father, it stifles the move of the Holy Spirit.

Displaying Proper Honor Prevents Outbreaks of Strife.

> *"But God composed the body, having given greater honor to that part which lacks it, that there should be no schism in the body, but that the members should have the same care for one another. And if one member suffers all the members suffer with it; or if one member is honored, all the members rejoice with it,"* (1 Corinthians 12:22-26)

Note the word "schism" in verse 25. God does not want fighting and disagreement in His church. When someone comes to you with words of trouble say: "Lets pray about this." Prayer is far better than discussing discord and strife.

Such behavior is actually the beginning point of the Body being what God really desires it to be. This keeps us from becoming selfish and isolated. It enhances the flow of the Holy Spirit in our lives.

Six Questions

"Now you are the body of Christ, and members individually. And God has appointed these in the church: first apostles second prophets, third teachers, after that miracles, then gifts of healings, helps, administrations, varieties of tongues. Are all apostles? Are all prophets? Are all teachers? Are all workers of miracles? Do all have gifts of healings? Do all speak with tongues? Do all interpret? But earnestly desire the best gifts. And yet I show you a more excellent way..." (1 Corinthians 12:27-31)

God, through Paul, poses six questions in this passage. The answer is most likely a resounding, "No." Even though God desires His people to flow in spiritual gifts and serve in ministry offices, far too many are missing out on their chance to function in these roles.

Not One, But Many

It is the desire of God that many people serve in leadership roles in the local church. Most congregations are not functioning to their highest level because of an overdependence on the pastor to do all of the ministry.

You may not be called to serve as a pastor, but you are called to function in some ministry role in your local church. Allow the Holy Spirit to guide you into your place of service.

"For in fact the body is not one member but many. If the foot should say, "Because I am not a hand, I am not of the body, " is it therefore not of the body? And if the ear should say," Because I am not an eye, I am not of the body," is it therefore not of the body? If the whole body were an eye, where would be the hearing? If the whole were hearing, where would be the smelling? But now God has set the members, each one of them, in the body just as He pleased," (1 Corinthians 12:14-18)

The unity within the Body of Christ cannot be found anywhere else on earth. After the 9-11 terror attacks in 2001, the U.S. seemed to be galvanized in opposition to the evil known as Al Qaeda. Inwardly I knew and verbalized it would not last. At the first sign of difficulty, strife would break out between the two political parties and sectarianism would again roar.

Sadly, I was correct. Our nation is more divided today than I have known it to be during my lifetime.

Division Is Not Inevitable

It is not necessary that the church be divided. We can flow in astonishing unity if we will properly discern the Lord's Body and flow in agreement with our role. If we are a "nose" we should be busy sniffing out what the Holy Spirit is doing on earth. If we are a "toe" we should be doing our part to support the foot by helping the Body of Christ to stand in faith.

Yes, we will see things differently, but we can flow as one in our areas of agreement. The world would be a better place if we were to see that we believe much more in common than what divides us. It is not necessary to give up what we believe in order to move in agreement.

Clarity Above All Things

Clarity Produces Kingdom Unity.

"And if they were all one member, where would the body be? But now indeed there are many members, yet one body. And the eye cannot say to the hand, "I have no need of you, nor again the head to the feet, "I have no need of you." No, much rather, those members of the body which seem to be weaker are necessary," (1 Corinthians 12:19-22)

We must honor, appreciate and edify each other in order to move freely in the gifts of the Holy Spirit.

A Tough Truth

The Holy Spirit spoke an uncomfortable truth to me in 1997. I was invited to lunch by a group of denominational leaders. I liked them and enjoyed their fellowship, but I saw the meeting for what it was: *a recruiting visit.*

I had no intention at all of becoming involved in their network. As I dressed for the meeting I said aloud, "I want nothing to do with denominationalism. This is pointless."

Draw A Bigger Circle

The Holy Spirit immediately spoke, "There was a time when men drew a circle and excluded you because of what you believed. Today I am requiring you to draw a larger circle to include everyone who includes Me."

As I entered the meeting, my heart melted. I saw these other preachers for who they were, men who loved God but were caught up in a time warp. Their experience was still revolving around where it started rather than going deeper in Him. My fellowship with them intensified over the years. In time many of them left their denominational fellowship, joined my network and declared me their Bishop. This all came about because God spoke and I obeyed.

The Power of Choice

Let us consider verse 13 again, *"For by one Spirit we were all baptized into one body-whether Jews (church people) or Greeks (unsaved people), whether slaves or free-and have all been made to drink into one Spirit."*

Regardless of where we come from, we all come to the Kingdom in the same way. We choose to drink the things of the Spirit. This choice moves us from outside the Kingdom to *into* the Kingdom.

Many Christians grow up in the church. Others do not. Yet each must be established in a place of honor and viewed as a candidate for the power of God to be displayed due to exercising the power of choice.

Brought Together by Difference

Many use our diversity as an excuse for strife. When I was younger, I relished the chance to debate the Bible with other believers. Looking back, I now know it had nothing to do with advancing the cause of Christ. It was all about my overwhelming desire to "be right".

1 Corinthians 11:29 encourages us to properly discern the Lord's Body:

> *"For he who eats and drinks in an unworthy manner eats and drinks judgment to himself, not discerning the Lord's body."*

When we really begin to see who we are in Christ we will be much less likely to engage in sectarianism. We will be much more inclined to love rather than engage in denominational and doctrinal debates.

A Controversial Truth

I know it is fashionable to preach that the Body of Christ will eventually speak the same thing and flow in great unity. I know this is the will of God, but it is unlikely to happen before the Millennial Reign of Christ. It is my belief that we will have to, instead, choose the way of love and simply agree to disagree.

For instance, I do not expect the Calvinistic Churches to give up their belief that everything is the pre-ordained will of God. Neither will I give up my belief that I serve a "right now" God of miracles.

Allow me to simplify. I spoke to Dennis, my brother, today. Our last name is Burton. That is not what makes us kin. Shared blood makes us kin. Richard Burton, the late actor, and I share a name but nothing more.

In the Body of Christ, we each have different last names. It is obvious we are not naturally related. Even so, we are blood kin. We share the blood of Jesus that has been applied to our lives.

A Strange Situation

We are incredibly different.

Yet, we are remarkably alike.

"For by one Spirit we were all baptized into one body-

whether Jews or Greeks, whether slaves or free-and have

all been made to drink into one Spirit..."

(1 Corinthians 12:13)

Chapter Six

Supernaturally Equipped

I was at a railroad crossing.

As I waited for the train to pass, I noticed something.

This was not the typical combination of cars hauling crude oil, automobiles and grains to market. This was a load of military equipment.

I sat in slack-jawed amazement as railcar after railcar of AH-64 Apache Helicopters passed before me followed by Bradley Fighting Vehicles and M-1A1 Abrams main battle tanks. This shipment had a far different mission than the rail cars that usually passed through my suburban crossing. This grouping was gathered for a specific purpose...*waging war.*

During the first Gulf War, not a single M-1A1 Abrams tank was lost in battle. Why? It was simply the best of its kind on planet earth. None of its descendants, the M-1A2, has been defeated, either.

When American forces go to war they are certain of the quality of their equipment. As a rule it is the best available. When armed forces go to war without fully functional weapons, the result is not nearly so good.

Jesus Was Fully Equipped

Famous people are not always correct.

One of my friends, a well-known minister, said something incorrect. He said we can expect to fail occasionally because Jesus failed. "If

God in the flesh can't heal everyone I will not have 100% success either," he said.

This is a misperception. It is true that Jesus had occasions where miracles were not prevalent. This had nothing to do with Him and everything to do with the faithless people to whom He was ministering.

Evangelical theologians claim we in the Spirit-Filled camp believe Jesus stopped being God.

No, we teach that Jesus set aside *(kenosis)*, poured out, His Divinity. He did not stop being God.

He stopped *functioning* as God.

He began functioning as a man empowered by the Gifts of the Holy Spirit.

Holy Spirit Basic Training

The most hated military experience is basic training. Yet, the most necessary portion of military training is basic. Soldiers cannot go on to Advanced Infantry Training without basic. This same analogy is true for the church. We must first master the basics, and God intends that we understand that His spiritual gifts are something He considers to be rudimentary.

The gifts of the Holy Spirit were given to the church as the weapons of our warfare. Too many believers are going to battle without their weapons and are being roundly defeated.

Two Reasons Jesus Came To Earth

1. Jesus came to earth to conquer sin and redeem lost mankind. He did this through being empowered by the gifts of the Holy Spirit. No matter what my well-meaning friend states, the totality of the ministry of Jesus was not done as God, but

as a man –functioning in the gifts of the Spirit.

2. All His miracles came about because of a gift of the Holy Spirit being in manifestation in the moment.

Can We Trust Jesus?

"He that believes on me, the works that I do shall he do also; and greater works than these shall he do; because I go to My Father," (John 14:12)

Evangelicals say we do not preach Jesus enough. They disagree with our emphasis on the Holy Spirit. I completely disagree with the criticism. My upbringing was filled with Jesus to the "nth degree." Yet, we cannot really know Jesus without the revealing ministry of the Holy Spirit.

The same Holy Spirit Who empowered Jesus is empowering us today. It is my belief the Bible teaches us we should be performing the same miracles Jesus performed the same way He performed them...*by the Power of the Holy Spirit.*

We Can Be Like Jesus

When I was a boy, the church sang a song called, "To Be Like Jesus." Our expressed heart cry was to be like Jesus. Yet, I believe the Bible teaches us we cannot be like Jesus without the power of the Holy Spirit, Jesus was never defeated and His Church, operating in His Holy Spirit, can live in complete victory, too. The only thing that can stop us is unbelief that comes through ignorance, bad teaching, or choice.

Everyone will not agree with you. they will be critical. Some will even lie. This passage proves people lied against the Apostle Paul:

"Now I, Paul, myself am pleading with you by the meekness and gentleness of Christ-who in presence am lowly among you, but being absent am bold toward you. But I beg you that

when I am present I may not be bold with that confidence by which I intend to be bold against some, who think of us as if we walked according to the flesh,"

(2 Corinthians 10:1-2)

Choose Your Clothing

We live in a flesh and blood world. Yet it is a world dominated by spirit beings. These spirit beings are released, or bound by choice. This warfare we fight is spiritual in nature...even it appears we are only walking through life.

"For though we walk in the flesh, we do not war according to the flesh," (2 Corinthians 10:3)

You will face battles while living out life. Because of this truth we must learn how and choose to do our fighting in the spirit realm through prayer and intercession.

Spiritual Warfare Defined

Spiritual warfare is not complicated.

Our emphasis in this warfare must not be on the demonic. Our emphasis must be upon a Holy God who destroys demonic strongholds. This spiritual warfare is not done in the natural, but must be focused on the spirit realm where we are destined to win if we will fight according to God's Word. Spiritual warfare is nothing more than sharply focused faith, intense, faith-filled intercessory prayer and bold declarations of God's Word, the known will of God.

"For the weapons of our warfare are not carnal but mighty in God for pulling down strongholds, 5 casting down arguments and every high thing that exalts itself against the knowledge of God, bringing every thought into captivity to the obedience of Christ,6 and being ready to punish all disobedience when your obedience is fulfilled, "

(2 Corinthians 10:1-6)

Spiritual Warfare Is Uncomplicated

It is not organizational. It is not programs and promotions. It is described in Zechariah 4:6:

> *"Not by might (an organization) nor by power (the decision of a board) but by My Spirit, says the Lord of Hosts."*

We are not fighting other people. We are fighting demonic structures. The gifts of the Holy Spirit are protective, but they are above all, offensive. The church is an army designed to take and hold ground.

Chapter Seven

Defining the Gifts

Gifts cannot be earned. They are called "gifts" for a reason. The fact they are "given" does not in any way minimize them. These gifts are not optional, as some might suppose. Some believe they are available on a "take it or leave it" basis, and there is some validity to that point.

Moving in spiritual gifts will not make you "more saved." However, choosing to omit their activity will find you living in less Kingdom power than you could have.

Our God is a Communicator

Without a stretch of the imagination we can say our God is the Ultimate Communicator. Because of this He has established the gifts of the Spirit as Divine Communications to flow through the person of the Holy Spirit. These gifts are to be transmitted to the local church to release the infinite power of the Living God.

God desires to communicate with His people. One of the ways He does so is through the manifestation gifts of the Holy Spirit.

Note the Power of Three

My spiritual father, Dr. Ron Smith, said, "The number of Divine perfection is three. Every perfect thing is stamped with the number three. Our Perfect God even stamped Himself with a three-fold revelation of Who He is and what He does."

The Godhead is composed of three members: the Father, the Son and the Holy Spirit. This is a clarifying example of the number three. *"For there are three that bear witness in heaven: the Father, the Word, and the Holy Spirit; and these three are one. And there are three that bear witness on earth: the Spirit, the water, and the blood; and these three agree as one,"* (1 John 5:7-8).

Mankind has been made in the image and after the likeness of God. *"So God created man in His own image, in the image of God created He him; male and female created He them,"* (Read Genesis 1:27).

This image is reflected in the truth we are a spirit, live in a body and communicate with earth by our soul.

"And the very God of peace sanctify you wholly; and I will pray God your whole spirit and soul and body be preserved blameless unto the coming of our Lord Jesus Christ,"

(1 Thessalonians 5:23)

Again, Dr. Smith, "The mark of Divine perfection is revealed in the gifts of the Holy Spirit. The divide themselves into three primary categories: revelation, power and inspiration. 3 + 3+ 3. Our God is perfect so we are describing Perfection + Perfection + Perfection."

Revelation Gifts

Our God is a communicator. He wishes to be known and to make His ways known on the earth. One of the ways He does this is through revealing something that man could not know by way of the sense realm. This form of communication is miraculous as mankind has no way of knowing this information except by revelation.

Seven of the nine Charismatic gifts manifest in the Old Testament. We see three of these gifts manifest pre-Pentecost in Matthew 16:16-17, *"Simon Peter answered and said, 'Thou art the Christ, the Son of the Living God.' And Jesus answered and said unto him, 'Blessed are thou, Simon Barjona: for flesh and blood hath not revealed it unto thee, but my Father which is in heaven.'"*

The revelation of Jesus as the Christ was both a word of wisdom and a word of knowledge. It was truth in existence in limited form and truth to come in universally available truth. Jesus declared the revelation as pure which was an act of discernment of the spirit (heart attitude) of Peter.

Within the revelation category are the word of wisdom, the word of knowledge, and the discerning of spirits.

Power Gifts

"This is the segment," Dr. Smith teaches, "where God imparts His Divine power and abilities into receptive man. These gifts of power release supernatural ability that no man on earth humanly possesses."

The category of power gifts includes the gift of faith, gifts of healing, and the working of miracles. The late Dr. Sumrall, renowned for his knowledge on this subject, says in his book the Gifts and Ministries of the Holy Spirit, "The *gifts* of healing is the only gift that has plurality." Later on we will explain why this is true.

Dr. Howard Carter received powerful revelation on the gifts of the Holy Spirit during the early 1900's. He described the gifts of the Holy Spirit as being "like a chain connected to each other." When we pull on one we often find we are making a demand upon all.

While we strive for clarity in understanding each gift, let me say they are often interrelated in their manifestation. This is especially true in the activity of the gifts of power.

Inspiration Gifts

In 1 Corinthians 12:31a the NKJV Bible tells us, *"But earnestly desire the best gifts."*

The best gift is the one you need to manifest most at the moment.

Because this is the third group, some readers may be tempted to think these are the "lesser" gifts. Such thinking is not remotely accurate. It is through this group God releases His anointing. This release of anointing stirs His church to walk in blessing.

It is popular in evangelical circles to say these gifts of prophecy, tongues and interpretation of tongues are only for private worship. While they can be used in private worship, they are clearly to be used for corporate edification. 1 Corinthians 14:3 describes the blessing released by these gifts as: "edification, exhortation and comfort."

Dr. Smith shares more insight on this topic. "Tongues and interpretation of tongues were not mentioned in the Old Testament. Because of this I declare these manifestations to be the Signature Gifts of the New Testament."

Dr. Sumrall publicly said, "These are the three most needed ministries in the church of the Lord Jesus Christ."

Defining the Gifts

Yes, I believe definitions are important. However, I believe an experience with the Holy Spirit is even more important. Some of these gifts are so linked we could best describe their activity as "a blended whole."

Some years ago I had a public dispute with a senior minister over ...you guessed it... definitions. He publicly disagreed with me, which was incorrect. But my caustic response was even more regrettable.

It is because of these truths, I want to encourage my reader and fellow ministers to"not bog down" over definitions. I have noted that arguments often blow up when two individuals are actually attempting to say the same thing.

There is a devil and he loves strife...*even strife over definitions.*

Through my years of ministry, I have made the acquaintance of many of the generals of the Faith. One of these men was Dr. Oral Roberts. During a conversation with him he casually stated, "People have often thought I moved in the gifts of healing. I won't dispute that, but I believe many of the most profound results seemed to take place when I moved in the gift of faith."

His point, although not deliberately made, is plain to me: results matter, not arguments over definitions.

Remain courteous and remember that entire denominations exist and separate millions of people because of definitions.

We will move into more detail on these gifts later, but let me offer brief definitions of each. While I have been profoundly influenced by Dr.'s Smith, Sumrall and Roberts, the following are my conclusions.

The Word of Wisdom: the revelation of the prophetic future under the anointing of God. I believe each Old Testament prophet who foresaw the future moved in this anointing.

My cousin, the late J. R. Goodwin, a close friend of Kenneth Hagin, was adamant that this was a "word" of God's wisdom. It is not a revelation of everything God knows on a subject. Think of the Word of Wisdom in terms of "foretelling." It is the revealing of an event before it happens.

The Word of Knowledge: the revelation of something in existence that can only be supernaturally known. There is no natural way of knowing this truth or set of facts.

Think of the Word of Wisdom in terms of "forth telling." It is a speaking forth of something that exists.

Again, the Word of Knowledge is about a fact that exists. The Word of Wisdom is about something that is to come.

The Discerning of Spirits: I agree with Dr. Smith; this is the revelation of the heart intention of a human more than the discerning of devils present. My way of describing this would be the revelation of the motivation of a person or spirit being.

The Gift of Faith: God brings supernatural things into being with no human effort. Someone believes and the supernatural happens.

The Gift of the Working of Miracles: a supernatural act by the power of God. Samson's bare-handed killing of a lion, as well as his lifting and carrying away the gates of a city, were the working of miracles because this human feat was done under the energy of the Holy Spirit.

The Gift of Tongues: a person proclaims a message in a public setting by speaking a language they do not understand. Because they do not understand the language, this act flows from the human spirit rather than the learned mind.

The Gift of Interpretation of Tongues: a person hears the tongue spoken in a public setting that is unknown by both the hearer and the speaker. The hearer then supernaturally interprets the message from heaven to earth.

Tongues and Interpretation of Tongues, again, were the only two of the nine gifts not manifest in the Old Testament. Because of this I agree with Dr. Smith that these are the "signature gifts" of the Holy Spirit.

Prophecy: the anointed speaking forth of words of edification, exhortation and comfort. It is fashionable in some circles to declare "there is no element of prophecy in the simple gift of prophecy." Huh? This is an incorrect teaching.

Each time the prophetic word goes forth in Scripture it is accompanied by promises for the obedient and penalties for the disobedient. Both these promises and penalties are predictive in nature, and therefore, prophetic.

Chapter Eight

The Word of Wisdom

I love Christmas.

Yes, I love celebrating Jesus.

But I also love something simple: gifts.

I delight both in giving and receiving gifts.

In this I am revealing the God nature within me. God the Father gave His best gift, Jesus our Savior. God the Son gave us His best gift, the blessed Holy Spirit. God the Holy Spirit gave us His best gift: His abiding presence.

We Are Discussing Gifts

These are gifts. They are not earned. They are not for an exclusive group. These spiritual gifts cannot be bought.

The manifestations of the Holy Spirit are given.

As we stated in the previous chapter, these gifts come in three categories: the Power Gifts, the Revelation Gifts and the Inspiration Gifts.

The Revelation Gifts

The Revelation Gifts are the Word of Wisdom, the Word of Knowledge and the Discerning of Spirits. In each of these cases information is shared from outside the natural boundaries for the purpose of making supernatural changes within the natural realm. This information is not seen with the eye; it is not imagined by the mind; this information is not heard by way of the ear. It is all supernaturally perceived and spiritually received.

The Word of Wisdom

The Word of Wisdom is supernatural information about something that does not yet exist within the natural realm. It can be considered to be both informative and predictive because God would have no reason to advise about a coming event if He had no insight into how to properly deal with that event.

Dr. Smith often described the Word of Wisdom as "a Divine foretelling."

One of the amazing things about Dr. Smith was his ability to see into the spirit realm. He would routinely tell someone about things to come.

One of these experiences caused me to seize onto a relationship that was transformative for me and the other person. He said, "God is bringing an unusual man into your life. He will be taller than you, a number of years older and will have a very strange laugh. God is sending Him to you for healing and acceptance. He will provide emotional appreciation to your family and be a strong financial supporter of your ministry. Do not disqualify him before discerning his heart. "

That individual did arrive, and he delivered a complaint about the first service he attended. He was so strange I wanted to withdraw from him, but I remembered the Word of Wisdom to receive him. At the time of this writing he has been blessing my family for many years.

The Word of Wisdom made the difference in this situation. Our acceptance of his strange ways allowed us to walk with him through a time of intense depression and suicidal tendencies after the death of his wife. Now beyond the age of 80, this brother is still productive in the workplace and in the spirit realm.

Dr. Smith was clear, "When God gives a Word of His Wisdom He is revealing something that does not yet exist. It may be a warning."

As I do not have the permission of her family to tell this story, I will not name the lady but can truthfully describe her as an amazing prophet of God who often moved in the Word of Wisdom. She told of family members who traveled to Minnesota each year to go moose hunting. One of the members who traveled with the group was a relative with the given name of Oswald.

In the fall of 1963 she began to pray against impending danger. Why? She heard the Holy Spirit say, "Oswald will be the shooter." She told everyone of what she had heard. Moved, they all pledged their diligence to be even more safety conscious than ever.

Upon their return, she was momentarily relieved. Even so, she told of how she was still troubled by what she had heard. She wondered if she had simply been victimized by her own imagination.

On November 23, 1963, she no longer wondered. President John F. Kennedy was assassinated during a campaign appearance in Dallas, Texas.

The shooter was Lee Harvey Oswald.

In 2013, God spoke to my spirit, "You will go back to small Texas towns like where you started. You will be blessed and be a blessing." I did not realize I would be returning because of brokenness. I thought I was going to lead the victory parade that my life had become. Instead I went back to be restored, and I did restore others during my process.

When I was in the fifth grade, after years of horrible violence, adultery and disrespect on the part of my biological father, my parents divorced. With nowhere else to go, Mom, Dennis and I moved into Granny Blum's 38 X 8 travel trailer with she and Papa Blum. To say it was beyond snug would be an understatement.

We moved to the tiny town of Plum Grove, Texas. The travel trailer was situated on the property of our home congregation, the Plum Grove Assembly of God Church. Fewer than two hundred people lived in the community. It was a difficult thing as my parents were described as being the first people to ever divorce there. Aside from our church, we were somewhat ostracized.

Because my father owned property there, the Splendora School District agreed to allow me to continue to attend school even though we had moved into an adjacent district. The school bus came within 2.5 miles of where I lived, so it meant a total of 5 miles of walking each day.

Living on the church property, after homework, I often went into the sanctuary to practice singing. One afternoon something amazing happened. While singing, I looked up and saw a man sitting between me and the back door. There was no way out but to walk past the man. I was frightened.

Attempting to keep my wits about me, I completed the song and casually began walking toward the door. Knowing what I know now, I saw the glory of God upon what looked to be a large, muscular, blue-eyed man. His head was lowered and he was weeping.

I hoped he would keep his head down, but it did not happen. As I neared him, he lifted his head, looked me in the eyes and said, "Malcolm, you are a blessing now, but you will be a far greater blessing in your later years."

Shocked and frightened more than I can describe, I ran for the door. Breathless, I burst into the trailer and told my grandparents of what had happened. They hurried out to the church. Papa looked inside while Granny looked in the three directions he could have driven. There was no one inside and no car in sight. Seeing how upset I was, they did not doubt something had happened, but they could not explain what had taken place.

Within minutes my Aunt Hazel Burton called. Hazel was a remarkable woman, a powerful intercessor with prophetic insight. She never traveled more than three hundred miles from her Plum Grove home, but missionaries routinely sent prayer requests to her. Because of this, I can truthfully say without stretching that her ministry literally reached around the world.

"Sister Lois," Hazel asked Granny, "Has something happened with Malcolm? Earlier this morning I had the sense he was going to have a powerful experience today."

Granny told her what had happened and Aunt Hazel said, "He just encountered an angel. He should not be afraid. He has received a message from God and must believe what he has been told." This was a manifestation of Aunt Hazel receiving a Word of Wisdom in the morning, information about something that did not yet exist.

As she spoke to Granny Blum by phone the Word of Knowledge came. My life changed in that moment. I thank God I had my now-deceased Aunt Hazel to interpret the moment for me.

The Holy Spirit is a Revealer.

He desires to inform us of things to come.

Dr. Smith taught me, "This gift is called the Word of Wisdom. It is not the totality of all God knows is going on. It involves speaking "spiritualities" or hidden things. This thing was hidden until God revealed it to your Aunt. Had she not been foretold of something exceptional coming your way, it may never have been interpreted correctly."

In 1 Corinthians 2:7 Paul teaches us, *But we speak the wisdom of God in a mystery, even the hidden mystery which God ordained before the world unto our glory."* These are things we would not normally know.

The Word of Wisdom gives God the ability to impart to us perfect knowledge of the future. As humans studying history, we cannot even begin to perfectly understand the future much less comprehend the past.

Today I received an offer of a "Daily Reading." It was a mass e-mailing from a lady who described herself as a "Medium." As I drive about I routinely see signs advertising fortune tellers, palmistry and tea-leaf readings. In the game room of a department store, I saw Ouija boards for sale. These things reveal a problem, and an incredible opportunity. Yes, these things are unscriptural. They exist because the church has failed in the realm of spiritual warfare, but they also present an opportunity for the church. This type of occult interest tells the church unknowing people are looking to hear from the supernatural realm.

Instead of disallowing public manifestations of the Holy Spirit as some churches are doing, we should be actively praying for more of this revelation outpouring. According to Jesus the problem is a simple one, *"You do not have because you do not ask God,"* (James 4:2).

If you desire revelation gifts to manifest, ask God.

Three Old Testament Examples
of the Word of Wisdom

The Prophet Joel had a Word of Wisdom when he prophesied of the outpouring of the Holy Spirit in the last days.

> *"And it shall come to pass afterward that I will pour out my spirit upon all flesh, and your sons and daughters shall prophesy, your old men will dream dreams, your young men shall see visions,"* (Joel 2:28)

In Chapter 53, Isaiah prophesies of the Messiah to come. By the Word of Wisdom he declares Him to be our Savior, Lord, and Healer. His description of the "stripes upon His back" that bought our healing was a Word of Wisdom. Such a type of punishment did not exist during the time Isaiah wrote of it.

New Testament Examples

Jesus did not function as God when He was on earth. No, I am not saying He stopped being God. He stopped functioning as God. How did He work miracles? Jesus functioned as a man moving in the gifts of the Holy Spirit.

Jesus moved in the Word of Wisdom in Matthew 24, Luke 21 and Mark 13 when He foretold the demolishment of the Temple. He prophesied many specific things that have already happened and others that are on their way to fulfillment.

God wants to reassure His people. When it looked like an angry mob would kill Paul, God gave him a Word of Wisdom. "Be of good cheer, Paul: for as thou hast testified of me in Jerusalem, so must thou bear witness of me also in Rome," (Acts 23:11). When it looked like he would never speak for God again, Holy Spirit stirred Paul's faith with a Word of Wisdom.

Paul moved in the Word of Wisdom when the ship he was on began to sink. He saw the solution by the Holy Spirit and told the sailors to eat some food to regain their strength, lighten the load and get ready to swim for shore. Just as Paul predicted in the Word of Wisdom, no one died.

Revelation Gifts Manifest in Different Ways

The Word of Wisdom was manifest in Joseph's life through a dream. Joseph was told his complete future. Special emphasis was placed upon the fact he would be a great leader and his brothers would bow down before him. As displeased as his brothers were, this truth came to pass.

Daniel received supernatural insight when the Word of Wisdom manifest to him in the form of a night vision. The Word of Wisdom that came to Daniel revealed much of the prophetic future of the time we are living in now.

Ezekiel and John were caught away and given the Word of Wisdom. Ezekiel saw Jerusalem being sacked by Babylonians. It happened. He was also caught away when he was given the Word of Wisdom that the Temple would be rebuilt.

John was caught away on the Lord's Day. The Word of Wisdom came to him and he received the entirety of what we know to be the Book of the Revelation.

Each believer is unique. Because of this, cultivate a willingness to allow God to reveal things to you in ways you have not considered.

On a July night in 1990, I received a spiritual dream. The setting was on the Merritt Island Wildlife Preserve near Cocoa Beach, Florida. I knew where I was because I could see Ron Jon's Surf Shop just to the South.

As I looked out into the Atlantic Ocean, I saw a huge wave coming toward the shore. Even though I awakened with hot tears on my face, I was not frightened by what I saw because I immediately interpreted the wave as a sign of the move of God coming to the United States.

Two things came out of that Word of Knowledge. I was able to accept without question the move of God when it came. The cry of my heart was, "Oh, God, don't let me die before that moves comes to America." I did not die and I saw that outpouring in the Brownsville Revival that brought renewal to so many preachers in the United States.

Something very personal came out of that powerful nighttime experience. I awakened with the knowledge that I was to start what became Northgate Family Church where I served for twenty-five years.

I Am So Thankful He Is A Revealer.

Chapter Nine

The Word of Knowledge

God is not holding out on you.

He desires to share life-changing insights. This knowledge brought about a step forward for me. It brought forth a huge step forward for the congregation I served.

We had owned some property on Interstate 45 for about five years. It had been a health and racquetball club that burned to the ground. Through a fabulous series of events, God gave us what we could not buy.

Our congregation wanted to build on the property and move our ministry to a more visible location. We cleaned the bushes off the property, repaired sidewalk and parking lot cracks, and generally did all we could without the money to really move forward.

Finally, the finances came together. We were ready to take a step forward when we were told by our architect the Harris County Engineer said that we could not build on the property because it was in the flood plain. Without a building permit, we could do nothing.

The disappointment was debilitating. I asked the architect to appeal. Instead, he gave me a final bill and encouraged me to sell the property for whatever we could get for it. "After all, something is better than nothing, and, as it sits, you have nothing, " he told me.

For weeks we did nothing but lament. One day while visiting with my Mom and Dad, Earl and Norma Sample, I saw a Federal Emergency Management Administration (FEMA) Map book with elevations for the part of Montgomery County where they lived.

They were interested in purchasing the house they were renting and Dad had brought the book home from work to check out the elevation of the property.

Since Northgate was literally located across the creek, I looked and found the church property described as being above flood level. I thought I had found the answer. The architect again told us he could not help, but he did send another bill.

Shortly after that, The Holy Spirit visited me during the night with the Word of Knowledge. "This is the day of favor," He spoke. Moved as I have been on few occasions in my lifetime, I called a dear friend and intercessor to agree with me in prayer.

"Surely," I thought, "the FEMA map is the answer." So, I announced to her my plans to drop in to visit the County Engineer of the most populated county in the United States without an appointment. She did not discourage me, instead she moved quickly into prayer. As we prayed she said, "Pastor, you will be escorted by the receptionist to a tall, grey haired man. He will be very kind, but he will say "No." Do not take his answer as final. Ask to speak with his supervisor."

The Word of Wisdom was manifesting for a second time. Not only was this the day of favor, God was describing a barrier and my way to walk around it.

She continued, "You will be taken to a man who immigrated to the US from another country. He will have a large book on his desk. He will give you the answer you are seeking."

FEMA Map in hand, I arrived to the office of the Harris County Engineer. I asked to see the County Engineer, but was told he was busy. I was taken to his assistant, a large, friendly man who quickly told me"No." I showed him the FEMA Map and was told we may have a case, but it would require court action.

I politely asked if there was anyone higher in authority I could speak with.

"The County Engineer is the only person with more authority here, but I believe he is busy. Let me see," he said.

"He has five minutes," I was told.

The Koran

When I entered his office I saw a man with a nameplate on his desk that contained a name I could not decipher. I also saw a large book: The Koran.

My heart sank. Even so, my human reasoning kicked in and I decided to show him The FEMA Map.

He quickly said, "I am familiar with this piece of property. Is there a building standing on it?"

"No, it burned," I replied.

"Oh, that is actually good. You don't need a building permit. You need a *rebuilding* permit. We can issue one today and you can go to work immediately."

Hallelujah! My heart thrills as I recall that day.

"I probably could have yielded based upon the FEMA Map," he said, "but, you would have to pay three percent of the estimated cost of the building for your building permit." I quickly calculated that to be near $9,000 which we did not have.

"However, since it is a fire loss, you will only need a rebuilding permit, and that is $500." The County Engineer handed me off to one of his assistants and I went away with a miraculous solution to a problem I had no natural answer for. The Word of Knowledge even permitted us to save money. What a great God!

"Papa Ron" and The Word of Knowledge

As I write this, I miss Dr. Smith intensely. "Papa Ron" was (and is and shall be) my spiritual father. Without him I would not be involved in the miracle ministry today. Heaven is richer because he is there, but earth is less a home to me because of his departure.

The gift of The Word of Knowledge deals with what exists. God is revealing something already in existence on planet earth.

"Papa Ron" often said, "We might more correctly refer to this as the Gift of the Word of God's Knowledge so we do not confuse it with man's wisdom." Knowledge refers to fact. This is something known that God chooses to reveal.

The gift of the Word of Knowledge deals with what exists.

Supernatural Protection

Dr. Smith and I were in his office at Coral Ridge Church. We were discussing the Houston Astros move toward the championship while wrapping up some accounting before a late lunch.

While I was around him a lot, the anointing upon his life continually astounded me. As we compared totals on a deposit he sharply spoke, "Evil just entered the property." Within seconds the door burst open and a distraught looking man came in.

"I have killed and I need prayer," he said.

Dr. Smith walked over, placed a hand on the man's shoulder and said, "Praise God! Lord, we thank for sending this man our way. Sir, you need help and we are going to give it to you."

Supernatural Utterance

The man began to sob about how he had killed and could not possibly be forgiven. Dr. Ron quietly prayed in tongues. Then he did something amazing. He turned to me and said, "Son, you have a question for the man."

Shocked beyond imagination, I opened my mouth to say "No." Instead I heard myself say, "You stopped using a .45 caliber pistol for a 9mm, because it was easier to get ammunition for it. Do you have the pistol with you now?"

The man laughed and said, "If I show you my gun will you show me yours?"

I said nothing. He reached inside his coat and pulled off his shoulder holster and laid it on the desk. It contained a 9mm Colt.

"Were you a field agent, " he asked. "Only a field agent would know to ask me that question."

Then the man began to sob uncontrollably and scream, "I have killed and there is no hope for me." The Word of Knowledge came to me again and I said, "The sin is not so much yours as those who assigned to you to kill others." He quickly confessed he was an assassin for an intelligence service.

It is not my goal to get into a discussion about just killing versus unjust killing. While I do not enjoy thoughts of violence I do recognize such is often necessary in protecting the inhabitants of our nation and its interests.

In this case The Holy Spirit gave me the words to say that started the man on his way to healing. He came into the office broken, but he left the office whole because the Word of Knowledge released healing into him.

Words of Knowledge from the Old Testament Prophets were imperfect. They were imperfect back then. Prophets are still imperfect today.

The great Prophet Elijah declared in 1 Kings 19:14 that he was the only real preacher alive. Not only that, but everyone on earth wanted to kill him because of his personal holiness. The Word of Knowledge came to the oppressed prophet: 7,000 other people were faithfully serving God in what appeared to be faithless Israel. Elijah knew nothing of this fact already in existence, so the knowledge had to flow from the supernatural realm.

Gehazi Goofs

Elisha followed Elijah as the major prophet of Israel. Elisha had a servant named Gehazi. History is unclear on Gehazi's function. He may have been an apprentice prophet, or simply what we would call an armor bearer. Whatever the position, Gehazi played a major role in the life and ministry of Elisha.

General Naaman, top man in the Syrian Army, came to visit Elisha. Plagued by leprosy, General Naaman was seeking healing. After receiving a miracle by simply bathing in the Jordan River, the very wealthy Naaman came to Elisha and expressed his desire to give him a gift.

Elisha said, "No, I don't want a gift. The best thing you can do to please me is to give The Lord glory for your healing."

Naaman did so and went on his way...*only to be followed by Gehazi.* "General Naaman, two young preachers arrived shortly after you left, " Gehazi said. "They are tired and in great need. Elisha sent me to ask if you can please send them some money and clothes." Thankful, Naaman did so.

Gehazi probably went back home feeling good about his scheme. What happened next must have overwhelmed him.

When he arrived back to the prophet's chambers, Elisha met him. "I know where you have been, Gehazi. Didn't you know my spirit was with you?" The Word of Knowledge revealed to Elisha where Gehazi had been.

Invest time in reading 2 Kings 6:8-12. The armies of Syria were coming against Israel. The Word of Knowledge came to Elisha. He sent word of their location to the King of Israel who dispatched troops and defeated the Syrians.

The Word of Knowledge came so many times the King of Syria said, "Someone among us is sharing secrets. A spy is giving our location to Israel."

Fearing for their lives, the soldiers said, "No, King. We are loyal. The truth is, there is a prophet in Israel who knows everything we are doing." The King James Authorized Translation reads,

"The prophet that is in Israel telleth the King of Israel the words that thou speakest in thou bedchamber," (2 Kings 6:12)

My prayer is that the Word of Knowledge will be in such manifestation in the church that people know prophets of God still walk the earth. My heart longs for society to know there is a God among us.

The Word of Knowledge worked mightily in The Prophet Samuel. Because of his dependence upon the Word of Knowledge, Samuel's ministry was so powerful it was said that *"None of his words fell to the ground,"* (1 Samuel 3:19)

In 1 Samuel 10 we see that God used the Word of Knowledge to reveal the location of King Saul when he went missing. Saul was a huge man. The Bible describes him as being the biggest man in Israel.

On the day of is coronation, Saul could not be found. A modest man at the onset of his rule, Saul feared the responsibility that came with being king. Samuel prayed and a Word of Knowledge came to him. Saul was *"hidden in the stuff,"* 1 SAMUEL 10:22. Saul was found, persuaded to come out and assume his kingly responsibilities. It all came to pass because of The Word of Knowledge.

The Word of Knowledge In The New Testament

Jesus moved in The Word of Knowledge. No, He did not function as God but as man. He functioned as a man flowing in The Holy Spirit.

The Woman at The Well is a familiar but not well understood story. In John 4 we see several unusual events took place on that day. Jesus went to the well at Noon and found someone there drawing water. This was unusual because of the heat of the day. The person he met was also out of the ordinary; a non-Jewish woman whom He spoke to. It was uncommon for Jews to interact with non-Jews, especially one who was a female non-family member.

The well was deep and Jesus needed help in getting a drink. He asked the woman to draw some water for him and began speaking with her.

Her response revealed the unusual nature of what was taking place. To paraphrase, she said, "Are you kidding? I'm a Samaritan. You are a Jew. Our people do not get along at all."

Jesus was determined to communicate with her. "I know all that, but the water I am offering you will cause you to never be thirsty again."

Her response was not a sweet one. Paraphrasing again, "Who do you think you are? Do you believe you are greater than Jacob? He dug these wells. This is good water. If you have water that is better than this, water I can drink and never be thirsty again, give it to me!"

"Call your husband," Jesus said.

"Can't be done. I don't have one," she said.

Jesus replied, "That is true. You have been married five times and the guy you are living with now is not your husband."

Fact after fact was revealed by the Word of Knowledge. Everything Jesus spoke was already in existence.

The woman was so excited she ran into the city and left her water pots behind. She said, "Come see a man who told me everything I have ever done." A rush of God's glory came to the city as people learned about Jesus.

Nothing is lost to God.

He knows the location of everyone and everything.

Activated By Prayer

The Word of Knowledge, like the other manifestation gifts, is often activated by prayer. In Acts 10:19 we see the story of Peter praying. The Word of Knowledge came to him, "Three men are looking for you."

As Papa Ron often told me, "God is always working on both ends." A man named Cornelius was praying"on the other end." As he prayed God spoke, "The man you are looking for is in the home of Simon the Tanner."

I have been to that house. It is still in existence to this day. I have been up on the roof where Peter received the vision of the sheet descending to earth with all kinds of food in it.

The Word of Knowledge continued to work. The Holy Spirit even went so far as to say, "Peter, the men who are looking for you are at the gate." The Word of Knowledge came to both Peter and Cornelius. This is the first record of The Word of Knowledge operating among Gentile believers.

The Word of Knowledge in Operation

I love Lola McIntosh

She is a Word of Faith Lady.

Recently, I ministered in Atlanta with Dr. Cassandra Scott. When I walked into the ballroom of The Crown Plaza Hotel, I saw Lola. She was clearly upset, an unusual state for one of the most joyous people I have known during my lifetime. Lola had misplaced her purse. All her cash and credit cards were inside. To make a rough thing worse, her Mom's check book, credit cards and cash were in the purse, too.

We all prayed for Lola during the service and declared she would recover all, just like God assured King David at Ziklag. I even went so far as to call her up to stand beside me and allow me to impart to her during my season of recovering lost things.

Even While Asleep

Something remarkable happened at 4:30am. The Word of Knowledge came to Dr. Scott, "Lola's purse is in your room." She arose from bed *...and found the purse next to the television.*

In October 2014, I was ministering at an International Church in Asia. One of the young ladies in the service looked distressed. As my compassion was stirred, a Word of Knowledge came and I spoke, "Something awful happened in your childhood that disturbs your sleep."

Tears began to flow as she told me, "My father attempted to have his way with me. I did not allow it and he slashed my face with a knife. He told me I would never be desirable to a man. I have been having the dream of him slashing me for months." Her college roommates testified that her screams had disrupted their sleep every night of the semester.

Under the inspiration of the Holy Spirit I called her classmates to gather around her and join their faith with my own. I then prayed a straightforward request for the peace of God to flood her mind. Deliverance came in that moment. Her classmates testified the next night that she (and they) had slept all night.

Freedom came because of the Word of Knowledge.

Not in the Delievery

In 1998 I was diagnosed with colon cancer. I was in a bad way when I was diagnosed. I did not respond to medical treatment and gradually sank into a more serious state.

Evangelist Gordon Jensen, my lifelong friend, was scheduled to be at Northgate on January 9, 2000. During the service Gordon quietly said, "A spirit of infirmity has attached itself to your body. I rebuke it in the Name of Jesus and call you healed and whole."

I grew up in Classic Pentecost. "Loud" is in my spiritual DNA. Gordon spoke quietly. It did not happen the way I expected, but my miracle came.

I was having blood drawn each week in order to estimate my condition. One week after Gordon spoke the Word of Knowledge, I discovered that, for the first time in months, my blood work did not decline. It stayed"flat" for a few weeks. Then it began to improve.

My physician told me three months later, "Mr. Burton, I no longer believe you are going to die."

Life came to me through The Word of Knowledge.

Chapter Ten

Discerning of Spirits

The Discerning of Spirits has no connection to anything natural.

It is not psychoanalysis, or extrasensory perception. It has nothing do with the mental realm, but of the spirit.

On far too many occasions I have heard this described primarily as a discerning of evil spirits. This is not the case. It is primarily understanding a human spirit —the motivation of the spirit within a person. This gift can operate in discerning three realms; the Divine, the demonic and the human.

Something This Is Not

This is not a conflict of human wills or human personalities vying for supremacy. It is not discerning who is right when spouses argue. It is also not *–no matter what Granny Blum thought–* the gift of suspicion.

What This Gift Is

Simply, this is the Divine ability to see (sense) or discern the presence or the activity of a spirit that motivates a human being. It is the Holy Spirit revealing the motivation of a human being as good or bad.

Let's consider this in the light of Hebrews 4: 12, *"For the Word of God is living and powerful, and sharper than any two-edged sword, piercing even to the division of soul and spirit, and of joints and marrow, and is a discerner of the thoughts and intents of the heart."*

We can see here the power of the Word of God working with The

Holy Spirit. The Word is living and powerful, and has the ability to cut (release access) into any realm by The Holy Spirit.

Note the conclusion: The Holy Spirit uses this gift as a discerner of the thoughts and intents of the heart. The discerning of spirits is especially helpful in choosing who should fulfill leadership roles within the body.

Simon The Soothsayer

Almost everyone desires recognition. This has always been true throughout human history and we discover this once again in the Bible accounting of the life of Simon the Sorcerer.

A soothsayer is a false prophet. Simon must have been making money through prophecy or some other form of Jewish ministry. *"And when Simon saw that through the laying on of the apostles' hands the Holy Spirit was given, he offered them money, saying, "Give me this power also, that anyone on whom I lay hands may receive the Holy Spirit,"* (Acts 8:18-19).

I grew up hearing, "Every man has his price." While I know this to be true of some, it is not true of all. Simon said to the Apostles, "That is a really cool gift. I will give you some money if you will give that gift to me. "

Peter's response was not exactly cool,

> *"But Peter said to him, "Your money perish with you, because you thought that the gift of God could be purchased with money! You have neither part nor portion in this matter, for your heart is not right in the sight of God. Repent therefore of this your wickedness, and pray God if perhaps the thought of your heart may be forgiven you. For I see that you are poisoned by bitterness and bound by iniquity"*

(Acts 18:20-23)

Almost no one has what Granny called "the gall" to really translate this verse correctly. Peter actually said, "To hell with you and your money."

Ignorance Among Greatness

Simon was observing the leaders of the early church. He saw what he knew to be signs, wonders and miracles. His motivation was not to help others; he wanted to make money off the gift of God.

Peter discerned, "You are full of bitterness and bound by iniquity." Why he was so filled with invective is unknown. He may have tried and failed in ministry.

The man who gave me the hardest time about financial matters was a pastor who had four churches close under his leadership. Except for a brief period, the church I founded always did well financially. After years of being oblivious, I learned the man had routinely questioned my financial integrity.

I wondered why I had not known of his activities. I questioned the working of the gift of God within me...*until I read about Simon.* He was in the midst of Peter and John during the glorious early days of the church. As spiritual as they were, no one recognized the evil at work within him until Simon opened his mouth.

My situation was similar. I did not recognize the mean-spiritedness of the failed pastor until he spoke harshly to me in a business meeting.

Good But Not Required

One group of people among whom I minister has a tradition of giving the prophet an offering after he/she speaks a word over them. While I don't mind the idea of a grateful soul blessing someone who ministers God's power to them, I have an issue with expecting an offering.

Essentially, prophets do two things: 1) share insights; 2) and release anointing. Something I have noticed is that the Holy Spirit often uses the prophetic utterance to"unlock" the people of God and move them in a desirable direction.

If such has happened in your life, you should be thankful. An offering would be a beautiful sign of your appreciation for the ministry you have received. However, you are not required to leave an offering afterward.

Elymas The Sorcerer

During the Old Testament a sorcerer was one who communicated with evil spirits and the spirits of the dead. By Paul's day sorcerers were known for introducing others into drug use to make them more receptive to spells and incantations.

In Acts 13 we see a pair of false prophets, Bar-Jesus and Elymas, working to keep a governmental leader in spiritual darkness. Victory over demonic spirits is not a work of the intellect. The Pro-Consul, Sergius Paulus, is described as"an intelligent man. "

We know Paul was a genius. But note that the Bible does not say, "Paul, a genius of a lawyer..." No, let's read it, "Then Saul, who also is called Paul, filled with the Holy Spirit, looked intently at him and said, *"O full of all deceit and all fraud, you son of the devil, you enemy of all righteousness, will you not cease perverting the straight ways of the Lord?"* (Acts 13:10)

Elymas probably appeared to be perfectly normal, but Paul saw the evil thing that was really working in him. Paul knew the motivation of Elymas by the power of the Holy Spirit through the Gift of Discernment of Spirits.

Beautifully Wrapped Deception

An attractive lady arrived to Northgate early one Sunday Morning. She sat quietly through praise and worship practice. When people greeted her she did not respond or so much as smile.

When I walked into the sanctuary she was facing the front of the building. It struck me as odd that she immediately stood and approached me.

"God has sent me here with a word of correction for this church," she boldly said. "I will await your signal for when it is time for me to speak."

In that moment, the discerning of spirits immediately manifest: I knew her motivation was not a good one. My statement to her was equally bold, "No, the only person with a corrective word for this congregation is me. You may sit quietly or leave."

She chose to leave quickly, with harsh words shouted on her way out. Thank God for His gift of the discerning of spirits.

Ananias and Sapphira

This husband and wife team were leaders in the local church. They became captivated by a man names Joses who sold all he had and gave it to the church. Apparently the church had a service of blessing and renamed him Barnabas.

They contrived between themselves to sell their property, keep back some for their own purposes, and give the rest to the church. The problem was that they lied about giving it all.

Apostle Peter had some powerful words for them.

"But a certain man named Ananias, with Sapphira his wife, sold a possession. And he kept back part of the proceeds, his wife also being aware of it, and brought a certain part and

79

laid it at the apostles' feet. But Peter said, "Ananias, why has Satan filled your heart to lie to the Holy Spirit and keep back part of the price of the land for yourself? While it remained, was it not your own? And after it was sold, was it not in your own control? Why have you conceived this thing in your heart? You have not lied to men but to God."

Then Ananias, hearing these words, fell down and breathed his last. So great fear came upon all those who heard these things. And the young men arose and wrapped him up, carried him out, and buried him," (Acts 5:1-6)

God Did Not Want All Their Money

Now it was about three hours later when his wife came in, not knowing what had happened. And Peter answered her, "Tell me whether you sold the land for so much?" She said, "Yes, for so much." Then Peter said to her, "How is it that you have agreed together to test the Spirit of the Lord? Look, the feet of those who have buried your husband are at the door, and they will carry you out." Then immediately she fell down at his feet and breathed her last. And the young men came in and found her dead and carrying her out, buried her by her husband. So great fear came upon all the church and upon all who heard these things," (Acts 5:7-11)

I am not advocating that people die during our church services. I am, however, sincerely desirous that The Gift of The Discerning of Spirits be operative in our local churches.

Two Powerful Quotes

"The gift of the discerning of spirits is a gift that enables one to appraise motives," –Lester Sumrall.

"The discerning of spirits is a gift of The Holy Spirit by which the possessor is enabled to see into the spirit world. By this insight he can discern the similitude of God, the risen Christ, the Holy Spirit, seraphim and cherubim, the archangels and the host of angels," – John Wesley.

We must have the Gift of the Discerning of Spirits in the church.

Chapter Eleven

The Gift of Faith

This chapter begins our study of the power gifts.

Most Full-Gospel scholars agree this grouping to be the second greatest aggregation of gifts behind the revelation gifts. The first of the power gifts we will study is the Gift of Faith.

We know from studying The Bible that there are many kinds of faith. The gift of faith is often mistaken for the simple faith necessary for us to receive salvation. However, the two are not the same thing.

"God has dealt to every man the measure of faith." (Romans 12:3). This is what I call *universal faith*. It has no relation to the supernatural sign gift of the Holy Spirit we are studying in this chapter. Clearly, there is a difference between the measure of faith, which The Bible says is given to every believer for use at their moment of salvation, and the gift of faith.

People of Natural Faith

Plum Grove, Texas is my home area. It has long been farming, ranching, timber and oil country. Each group contained strong believers who impacted my life, but in this moment I am thinking of the faith of the farmers. While speaking with my Dad, Mr. Earl Sample, Sr., a successful soybean farmer; he said, "It never once occurred to me to wonder if the seed would produce a harvest."

As spiritual as that sounds to those who understand the law of sowing and reaping, it is also a description of natural faith. Dad believes the seed will go into the soil, rain will fall from the clouds, and a harvest will spring forth as a result.

While I was in China I observed professional fishermen who constructed fishing "pens". These were walled enclosures that would be covered by Pacific Ocean waters at high tide. Without fail, when the water receded the fishermen went to the beach in expectation of a harvest. Their part was to build the wall and collect the fish, both acts of natural faith.

Saving Faith

From the spirit realm flows something called "saving faith."

When someone hears the message of the gospel and believes the promises of Jesus to be true, they are born again. They are saved as a result of saving faith.

Every born again person on earth has experienced the power of saving faith. However, not every person has the gift of faith.

Two Examples of Saving Faith

Luke 23:34-43 explains the story of the thief on the cross next to Jesus who displayed saving faith and was born again. He did not know enough to expect a manifestation of the gift of faith, but saving faith did bring him to the place of believing on Jesus to be saved.

The Philippian jailer prostrated himself before Paul and Silas. He asked the question that changed his life forever: *"Sirs, what must I do to be saved?" And they said, Believe on the Lord Jesus Christ, and thou shall be saved,"* (Acts 16:30-31). The jailer received the counsel, moved in saving faith and came into The Kingdom of God.

The Greek word for saved is *sozo*. The late P. C. Nelson taught it to mean, "Delivered from past, present and future sin, sickness and calamity." Because of this insight I believe healing manifests through saving faith. Three times in the Book of Luke 7:50; 17:19; 18:42) Jesus said faith had saved (healed) a sick person from sickness and disease.

The Gift of Faith Is Different

The gift of faith does exploits that cannot be done by human means. God, through the Holy Spirit, does supernatural things that cannot be humanly explained.

> "If these exploits can be done ordinarily, by human means, they have no relationship with the Holy Spirit."

> –Dr. Ron Smith

> "The gift of faith has to do with the functioning of God in you and through you, but with no human strength involved."

> –Dr. Lester Sumrall

Protection and Provision

The gift of faith can bring about divine protection and divine provision. It works independent of you. Again, all you do is believe.

Our church was in a tight financial spot. One Friday afternoon I sat in the church office and wondered how I would manage to pay the staff and keep the lights on. Instead of speaking lack I declared the promise of Philippians 4:19, "I believe You are a provider, and You will meet all my needs through your riches in glory by Christ Jesus."

My office door opened to the parking lot, but was covered by shrubbery. I heard a knock. As unusual as it was, I opened the door and found a teary-eyed young man staring at me.

He said something amazing. "My name is Daniel. I am a backslider. As I drove by this building I heard God say, "Pay your tithe."

He handed me a check for $8,000. It was the first of many times God used the man to bring miraculous provision to our congregation.

Jesus spoke to the storm and it stopped. This was the gift of faith in operation. I had a similar experience with a pastor I served when a tornado was approaching the church property. He commanded the storm to bypass us and it did. That was the gift of faith operating in him, too.

Both examples contain the same thing: the people did nothing but believe.

A Visit to the Fountain

I have visited the"Fountain of Youth" discovered by Ponce De Leon in what is now San Augustine, Florida. I went along with the joke of drinking the awful tasting water. I don't believe it had much of an effect. Yet, I have tasted of a different fountain, the fountain of faith, and it is still providing and protecting for me to this day.

At age 11 a powerful revelation came to me as I stretched out, reading on my grandfather's bed on a hot autumn Sunday afternoon in the insufferable heat and humidity of the Big Thicket of Texas. *The Pentecostal Evangel* was a staple in their house, and I read an article that afternoon on the topic of Christian Meditation.

"I remember thee upon my bed and meditate on thee in the night watches," (Psalm 63:6). In that moment I was captivated by the thought that I routinely did that. I was meditating on the ability of God.

Today, I understand that this sort of meditation is a preparatory key to understanding the ability of God that flows through the gift of faith. It was during this time that I began understanding the need to trust the ability of God rather than attempting to do supernatural things alone.

Nikon -vs- Hupernikon

In the natural we can conquer. In this we demonstrate nikon, or victory. When we move in the gift of faith we demonstrate hupernikon. We move from being victors to being recognized as super victors.

Dr. Sumrall was known to use a telling illustration based on

Romans 8:37: "A conqueror is a person who meets another person of equal strength and knocks him out. A person who is more than a conqueror just speaks and the other person falls down!"

When we close our hands in the natural realm and move in the gift of faith, God opens His hands in the sprit realm. Miracles then flow from the spirit realm into the natural realm.

Chapter Twelve

The Gifts of Healings

"To another gifts of healings by the same Spirit..." (1 Corinthians 12:9) We are continuing our study in The Power Gifts.

Two things before we go deeper: You are not seeing a typo; the proper explanation of this gift is in the plural form. This explanation is controversial to those who believe the day of healing and miracles is past, and to those who object to the plural aspect of the definition.

The Gifts of Healings defined: The supernatural power of God used to heal all kinds of illness without medicine or any kind of human remedy.

The Gifts of Healings have always been part of God's plan for the New Testament Church of Jesus. This was prophesied in Isaiah 53:5: *"But He was wounded for our transgressions, He was bruised for our iniquities; the chastisement for our peace was upon Him, And by His stripes we are healed."*

Jesus paid the price for healing from every disease known and unknown to mankind. A number of highly trained medical personnel have told me there are 39 categories of disease. Jesus was lashed 39 times with a Roman whip called "the Cat of Nine Tails."

An Established Fact

The Apostle verified the truth of his own writings. *"Who Himself bore our sins in His own body on the tree, that we, having died to sins, might live for righteousness-by whose stripes you were healed,"* (1 Peter 2:24).

It is my belief that any believer can be healed by believing and speaking the Word of God. Another quick way of moving against sickness is through the prayer of agreement.

However, there seem to be situations where we need the help of a spiritual specialist to see our mountain of ill health be moved. I believe it is during this time that our God desires to use a man or woman in the area of one of The Gifts of Healing.

Areas of Greater Success

If you have been attentive you have probably noticed that those who flow in healing seem to have areas where they have greater success. The late Charles Hunter, husband of Frances, was part of the powerful Happy Hunters. Their daughter, Joan, has continued in their healing legacy and is an amazing minister in her own right.

Charles Hunter had a profound level of faith for people who had suffered back injuries or had some sort of natural infirmity in that area. When I served as a pastor and was unable to get someone healed of some sort of back issue, I sent them to Charles and Frances. I do not recall a single time that individual came back unchanged.

Healed of Colon Cancer

Gordon Jensen has been my friend for more than forty years. He has served God as a great singer and award winning songwriter with ten Dove Award Nominations, symbolic of the best in Christian Music, to his credit. He also flows as a prophet of God with a dynamically productive healing ministry. My miracle validates Howard Carter's point that when we pull upon one spiritual gift others often manifest, too.

On January 9, 2000 Gordon came to minister in the Sunday Services of the church I served in Houston. I knew my friend had been flowing in a fresh anointing, but I had no idea of what was to come.

I had been diligent to soak myself in the Word of God. I had attended the meetings of the people with respected healing ministries, yet I was still in a bad place and sensed life was escaping me.

A number of things happened that morning, not the least was my best friend being healed of acute scoliosis. From across the room I heard the"pop" sound as her spine aligned. She immediately began to move about with a degree of freedom she had not had just moments prior. The constant pain she had suffered since she was age 11 was gone.

An Unusual Anointing

I did not know it before the service began that day, but God was already using Gordon in healing a number of different challenges with cancer being one of them. Actually, the first miracle God worked through him came as a result of a Word of Knowledge about an unborn child who was diagnosed with brain cancer. He spoke the healing word. Present that night in Memphis, TN was a mother who had been advised that afternoon to abort her unborn child due to a"huge" brain tumor. The mother refused the abortion and the child was born whole. It has been 16 years since the event and the child remains completely healthy in every way.

By the time he arrived to Houston, Gordon was well-established in faith that God would use him in the Word of Knowledge to minister in the gifts of healings to the sick. He already had remarkable faith that cancer would bow before the resurrected Christ.

Not What I Anticipated

Immediately after the miraculous touch of God that eradicated scoliosis, Gordon got my attention. He spoke in a normal voice devoid of any emotion of any kind, "Pastor, God spoke to me on the flight down here. He said you are bound by a spirit of infirmity. I rebuke it in the Name of Jesus and it must go."

My congregation loved me and they shouted in praise. I felt no better and could only muster a weak smile. I was seeking God for healing and wanted to be made whole. However, I had an expectation of how it would happen...*and that was not it.*

Inwardly I thought, "That's all you have?" Pentecost. "Loud" is in my spiritual DNA. If it's something miraculous I *knew* it had to be loud.

Benny Hinn loudly said, "Let it be so!"

Charles and Frances Hunter praised God in advance.

Legendary Evangelist Oral Roberts jerked my head around and declared me whole, "In the Name of Jesus Christ of Nazareth!"

My Canadian friend softly called it done...*and it was.* As I wrote earlier, soon I had the first blood test that did not show worsening symptoms. I stabilized for a few weeks before moving toward manifest healing.

The Gift in Dr. Ron Smith

Compassion is a Powerful Spiritual Motivation. Due to the deafness of a favorite cousin, Dr. Smith had remarkable compassion for the deaf. He would pray for anyone about anything, but he had a special heartbeat for those who had hearing challenges.

I do not recall him ever having a hearing-challenged person ask for healing to go away lacking. He would take time to establish the individual could not hear, and then would minister healing and painstakingly prove the work of healing had been done.

Something Out of Nothing

During a five-week outbreak of revival with Evangelist Jeff Taylor, we saw amazing things happen with hearing impaired individuals. A number of people who were hard of hearing went away hearing a full range of sounds.

Thunderstorms on the Texas Gulf Coast are not unusual. One night during the revival the lights went out due to the violence of the storm. Our ushers got together flashlights and we continued the service.

We were never able to get the lights restored. But, our God was already at work in the restoration business.

Two ladies sensed their faith rising and came forth. One was a 17-year-old and the other was a pastor in her early 40's. The teen had been born with no hearing mechanism and had been given an implant to enable her to hear. She testified to being touched by God that night and went off with the youth group. When she came back from camp she gave an unusual testimony.

"When I went to camp before I usually got more rest than everyone else because I could turn off my device, hear nothing and go to sleep. This time, no matter what I did, I could hear everything."

The pastor had developed what was known as a"Super Ear". The functional ear overcompensated to the point where she had almost a complete level of hearing. On that evening she felt the Holy Spirit nudge her to go forward.

Through the gift of healing, God did a creative miracle and the pastor is now able to hear as well out of the left ear as she does with the right.

Gifts of Healings in My Ministry

The gifts of the Holy Spirit are given for the benefit of all. It is because of this I feel the urge to point out that the gifts will move in harmony with each other. I have seen great works of God that brought healing through the movement of the gift of faith.

I have also had time when gifts of healing were flowing in specific areas. I knew this because I had unusual faith for specific things in that moment. I do not believe God had a specific desire to do some supernatural healing and restoring work above another. No, He knew the need present and stirred my faith in that area.

Robert Arevalo is one of my spiritual sons. He leads the great Grace Family Church in San Antonio, Texas. A former Navy Corpsman, Pastor Rob took care of wounded Marines in battle. He is an amazing man.

During a time of ministry there, Pastor Rob's mother came forward asking for her eyesight to be restored. She had just been to The University of Texas Health Science Center School of Medicine in San Antonio on the Friday afternoon before we were in service together on Saturday Night.

Great faith rose within me. I declared her whole and she went on her way in expectation that God would keep his promise.

Two months later I went back for another round of revival meetings. Sister Arevalo came forth to testify. "The physicians told me I was going blind. They said my only hope was an experimental type of eye drops they gave me that day."

I went back a week later and they were incredibly excited, "We have found a cure for this disease! After using these eye drops for a week, your eyesight has returned to normal."

In the next moment they were crushed because she said, "I thank you for what you did, doctor. But, I never used a single eye drop. I attended a revival service at my son's church and God healed me. "

Why I Believe in Multiple Gifts of Healings

Jesus is the only person to operate in the healing ministry with 100% success. I cannot find a single instance where Jesus was unable to heal someone who desired to be healed.

Paul was not 100% successful in healing the sick. For that matter, some of those close to him were left behind because they were sick (2 Timothy 4:20).

Simon Peter, the first Bishop of Rome, could not get his mother-in-law healed and had to ask Jesus for help (Matthew 8:14-15).

I will unashamedly say God uses me in the healing ministry and I am thankful for this truth. However, as a pastor I came to understand that I was the *family practice physician* of the local church. On occasion a *specialist* is needed to minister to the Body.

I believe God does not desire to manifest all His ability through one person. Consider Isaiah 42:8, *"I am the LORD: that is My name: and My glory will I not give to another..."*

If one person functioned at such a level as to heal everyone, that person would be esteemed too highly. I believe an unimaginable number of people would consider that person to be God. No one person could handle the adoration, praise and financial blessings that would come with being able to heal every disease.

God reserves His glory for Himself.

He will not share His glory with another person.

Chapter Thirteen

The Gift of Prophecy

God wants His people to be strong.

He wants us moving in the power of His Spirit.

He wants us informed about what is to come so we live in victory.

The three gifts of inspiration, prophecy, tongues and interpretation of tongues are meant to shape the believer so the church can shape the world. These gifts are for the benefit of the church and release three areas of ministry: edification, exhortation and comfort.

Maturing Gifts

Flowing in these gifts is meant to mature the church. A mature church is one that is alive unto God and powerful in its actions on planet earth. These gifts produce a church that is different from what many believe Christianity to be today. It is not one that is constantly questioning the will of God, but one that is consciously doing the will of The Father.

An Axe to Grind

Yes, I do have "an axe to grind." It is fashionable today to say there is no "supernatural component within the gift of prophecy." Amazing. These folks amaze me. Why? Because they are amazingly wrong. If the gift of prophecy is one of the gifts of the Holy Spirit it is, by nature, supernatural.

Look back upon what I taught about the Word of Wisdom and the Word of Knowledge. Much of what people call "prophecy" today is actually a Word of Knowledge with an instruction attached, or a Word of Wisdom structured in the same way.

I Disagree with My Mentors

I was taught the gift of prophecy is not predictive. Respectfully, I disagree. Please hear me out on this.

A prominent mentor of mine told me the prophetic (predictive) word can only flow through a prophet. That had not been my experience.

More often than not these prophetic directions flowed in the form of a Word of Knowledge or a Word of Wisdom revealing a path to take.

A 4AM Phone Call

I agree that the prophet is one of the five-fold ministry offices revealed in Ephesians 4:8-12. I agree with their assertion that a prophet is a person, not a vocal gift. He ministers from the office of the prophet.

However, I do not agree that only a prophet can prophesy. I believe the problem is in how we define prophetic ministry.

Please engage with me here. Dr. Smith called my home at 4AM. I was scheduled to meet with a renowned minister later that day to interview for a position on his staff as a writer/editor. Dr. Smith wept as he told me, "God told me to give you up to this man's ministry." He did not tell me everything else he had heard through the Word of Wisdom.

I wept all day. The thought of leaving my spiritual father brought a level of pain I could hardly bear. My emotions were so wrecked that I put ice packs over my eyes during the early afternoon in an effort to make myself presentable.

At 6PM I walked in the office of Dr. John Osteen to meet someone I will not name here. The gentleman was gracious and expressed enthusiasm over the idea my joining his staff. I answered the man's questions and was offered a position, which I accepted.

A Sudden Change

It was all I could do to keep from crying. I needed to support my family, but moving out of state was more than my Texas loving heart could bear. Worst of all was being distanced from my pastor.

My new employer looked across Pastor Osteen's desk with a quizzical expression. "I am a Southern boy," he said, "just like you. I do not like where my ministry is headquartered, but I have been there too long to easily relocate."

Then he said something amazing. "I am not going to ask you to move to my city. I want you to travel with me in the U.S. and we will work together on the road."

The flow of favor continued. These were days before the internet made remote editing a relatively easy thing. Then he said, "We can correspond by sending our documents through FedEx."

The Rest of the Story

As soon as I was released from the meeting that night I stopped at a pay phone to call Dr. Smith. I told him what had happened. He gasped aloud and said, "Let me tell you the rest of the story."

"God spoke to me this morning to let you go." Dr. Smith continued, "If you do, I will give him back to you and a river of blessing will flow that sustains both of you."

The fact you are reading these words in book form is proof of the accuracy of this predictive "word" from the Lord. It was a Word of Knowledge flowing with a Word of Wisdom. It did prophesy my future.

Three Things Prophecy Is Not

1. **Prophecy Is Not Just Preaching.** Those rooted in

Calvinism today will often declare that the only form of prophecy on the earth today is preaching. It is only through preaching, they say, that the will of God is made known. I do believe prophetic preaching to be a valid exercise of the gift of God. David Wilkerson was a preaching prophet during my lifetime. Dr. Kenneth E. Hagin is a great example of a teaching prophet.

2. **Prophecy Is Not Used To Rebuke People.** One of the common problems of today is New Testament ministers attempting to function as did Old Testament Prophets. On countless occasions the Holy Spirit has revealed the sin of someone present to me while preaching. Not once have I pointed out that person's error. Once when I shared this belief, a sanctimonious person came to me in an attempt to correct me. "Nathan told King David, 'Thou art the man!'" Take a moment to read 2 Samuel 12:7. They were in the private part of the palace. Nathan did say the world would know of David's sin before dark. Yet, this was not apparently the way things worked out because of David's repentance. Everything we do in ministry must be done in the light of the new and better covenant described in Hebrews 8:6.

3. **Prophecy Is Not a Vehicle We Drive to Criticize Others.** One of my mentors would say the gift of prophecy is not predictive, but then claim God used it to warn men and women of sin or shortcomings. You can tell from point two why I find his thought to be inconsistent. Prophecy is always positive when manifest properly. "The gift of prophecy can be used to lift a Christian out of his depression, his negligence, his lukewarm-ness, and put him back into the mainstream of the thrust of God," -- Dr. Lester Sumrall.

Three Things Prophecy Is

Prophecy manifests for three reasons:

1. **Edification.** A word often used to describe a building is edifice. P.C. Nelson taught edify means "to build up." In its root meaning it means to erect, strengthen or build up. It removes weakness from the spiritually struggling. It removes fear from the fearful. On a routine basis I meet people who need to be built up and strengthened. There is no doubt in my mind Paul spoke in tongues more than anyone alive because I believe the Bible is true. Paul wrote, *"I thank my God I speak with tongues more than you all,"* (1 Corinthians 14:18). Edification is critically important. It is one of the reasons I believe we should seek to prophesy.

2. **Exhortation.** Encouragement is a key element of prophecy. Exhortation often encourages someone to get busy for God because of His desire to bless the obedient. When I was a young boy, Pastor Rayburn Gilbert spoke over me, "You will travel the earth in ministry. You will be renowned as a singer, preacher and teacher." I saw that come true early in my lifetime. During the darkest season of my life I reminded myself of this exhortation. Encouragement came every time. Each time you exhort someone to go forward in God, you are engaging in prophecy because of the implication of implied blessing.

3. **Comfort.** The next time you are out, look at those around you. You will be astonished by the number of people who need consolation. Barnabas is one of my favorite Bible characters because of his name. It means "Son of Consolation; Son of Exhortation; Son of Comfort." Give people the comfort of a prophetic promise of better days.

The church is in the world but not of the world. The church needs

the comfort of the Holy Spirit to flow.

Without even recognizing it, we routinely meet people who do not

know what to do next. They are so confused they are considering

suicide. These people need prophecy...edification ...exhortation

...comfort.

Dare to prophesy to those you love and those you meet who are

suffering. Say, "Be edified, exhorted and comforted. God is for you."

Chapter Fourteen

The Gift of Tongues

There is much confusion on this topic.

Seven of the nine Charismatic gifts are in operation in most churches.

However, diverse tongues and the companion gift of interpretation of tongues are refuted by much of "mainstream" Christianity. They claim these two gifts disappeared with the death of the last apostle. They also claim healing is not for today, but embrace prophetic preachers.

Truth be told, these folks will go to almost any length to explain away the lack of power in their gatherings. They claim evil happenings to fall under the mysterious will of God, and claim He is teaching through circumstance. This same group will embrace their Calvinistic leanings and proclaim any desirable thing that fails to come to pass as being part of the pre-ordained will of God.

Note The Distinction

In this chapter I am not teaching about the tongue of initial evidence which manifests at the time an individual is filled with the Holy Spirit. I am also not referring to the devotional tongue that comes with this experience, but a manifestation gift which must be mastered.

Seven of Nine Is Not Enough

Seven of the nine Charismatic gifts flowed in the Old Testament assembly. The only two that did not manifest were the same two that critics claim should be absent today, tongues and interpretation of tongues.

"Again, tongues and interpretation of tongues are the Signature Gifts of The New Testament Church age." –Dr. Ron Smith

The Great Howard Carter

Howard Carter, a native of Birmingham, England, received the revelation of The Gifts of the Holy Spirit while imprisoned as a conscientious objector during World War I. It is an accepted fact that the whole of the Pentecostal/Charismatic movement embraces the doctrines he developed and established while leading Hampstead Bible School from 1921-1948.

"Therefore tongues are for a sign, not to those who believe but to unbelievers; but prophesying is not for unbelievers but for those who believe," (1 Corinthians 14:2). Brother Carter taught, Dr. Smith continued to teach, and I still teach, "Tongues is a sign gift to stir the thoughts of the unbeliever."

One of Two Unique Gifts

Tongues is unique to the church age.

Carter taught speaking with tongues as the Holy Spirit gives utterance (the ability to speak) is a unique ministry that was not used in other dispensations. This is the age in which we live today.

This activity was initiated on the Day of Pentecost, the birthday of the church, as described in Acts 2. Contrary to Calvinist teaching, none of the Charismatic Gifts, including tongues and interpretation of tongues, has ever left the church. None of these gifts has an expiration date.

Dr. Sumrall, a protégé of Brother Carter, taught tongues as a sign gift. Dr.Sumrall shares in his book, *The Gifts and Ministries of The Holy Spirit*, "This supernatural utterance comes from God through the person of the Holy Spirit. This remarkable gift is directed through man's spirit and manifests as a spirit language, a divine and spiritual communication that is different from his native tongue."

One of my beloved friends, Evangelist Joe Jordan of Shawnee Mission, Kansas makes a profound observation. "Every kingdom has a king. Our King is Jesus. Every Kingdom has a language. The language of our Lord's Kingdom is tongues."

The Most Misunderstood Gift

No gift receives such a profound reaction as the gift of tongues in operation. Tongues cause satan so much grief he does what he can to stir trouble and get people to fight over the issue. If tongues were the non-issue some churches claim it to be Satan would not fight the manifestation of this gift nearly so much.

Jason, my youngest son, was an Army Ranger. The most peace-loving of my children developed into a warrior. It was interesting to me to listen to he and "Paw Paw" (my dad, Mr. Earl Sample, Sr.) tell of the days of instruction before dad was allowed to operate the B.A.R., or Jason got to fire an M-4 rifle. Both were required to understand in detail the capabilities and operation of the weapon before they were allowed to use it.

Things are much the same for the church with the gift of tongues. We need to understand this "weapon of warfare" before we attempt to use it. It was not enough for Jason or dad to use his weapon. Each was required to develop proficiency.

Things operate the same way in the Kingdom. We must be capable in every area of ministry. This is true, too, with the gift of tongues.

Four Things the Gift of Tongues is Not

1. As I shared earlier, the gift of tongues is not the tongue of initial evidence that comes when one receives the fullness of The Holy Spirit.

2. Tongues is not the prayer language that comes with the infilling of the Holy Spirit as described as in Acts 2:4.

3. Tongues is not a learned thing. You may and should become proficient in such an exercise, but the gift of tongues has nothing to do with natural knowledge. It is a gift of the Holy Spirit, not a developed facility for language shaped in a university setting.

4. Tongues is not speaking from understanding. "For he who speaks in a tongue does not speak to men but to God, for no one understands him; however, in the spirit he speaks mysteries. For if I pray in a tongue, my spirit prays, but my understanding is unfruitful," (1 Corinthians 14:2; 14).

Who Qualifies for This Gift?

Spirit-baptized believers qualify to manifest this gift. The infilling of the Holy Spirit is the bridge into the supernatural and the operation of the spiritual gifts. The operation of the spiritual gifts, including the public ministry of tongues is on the other side of this bridge.

During my ministry lifetime I have encountered many who do not wish to operate in the supernatural. This is an unacceptable position. Consider what Paul wrote under the inspiration of The Holy Spirit, *"I wish you all spoke with tongues, but even more that you prophesied; for he who prophesies is greater than he who speaks with tongues unless indeed he interprets that the church may receive edification,"* (1 Corinthians 14:5).

Who Is Exempt?

There is no doubt in my mind Paul spoke in tongues more than anyone alive because I believe the Bible is true. Paul, our ministry prototype, wrote, *"I thank my God I speak with tongues more than you all,"* (1 Corinthians 14:18).

One of my dear brothers was in the Reformed Church. He loved me and appreciated my ministry as I did his. He was part of a denomination that believes the supernatural no longer exists. When I encouraged him to go deeper and experience the power of the Holy Spirit he said, "I'm not one of you. That is not for my church."

Jesus only has one church. Jesus commanded us to become proficient in tongues.

> *"And He said to them, go into all the world and preach the gospel to every creature. He who believes and is baptized will be saved; but he who does not believe will be condemned. And these signs will follow those who believe: In My name they will cast out demons; they will speak with new tongues;"*

> Mark 16:15-17

The verses above state the position of Jesus. Can we trust Him? I believe we can. His history is one of speaking truth. Because Jesus spoke this, no one is exempt from this command.

New Testament Church Model

Those who know me understand that I am a flexible individual. I am not interested in rigidity in my dealings with other people. However, I will adhere to the Word of God.

In this verse we are given the elements of a New Testament church service, *"How is it then, brethren? Whenever you come together, each of you has a psalm, has a teaching, has a tongue, has a revelation, has an interpretation. Let all things be done for edification,"* (1 Corinthians 14:23).

Unifying, Not Dividing

I served as Senior Pastor of a church in the North Houston, Texas suburb of Spring. Each year the merchants of Old Town Spring, the ultimate tourist trap, would host a parade. Our church would participate by passing out candy, soft drinks and gospel tracts.

One year we were distributing a book called *Why Tongues?* Written by Kenneth E. Hagin, it is a marvelous advocacy of Spirit baptism.

As we prepared to distribute these books along with a number of other publications we believed would bless the readers, a Calvinist pastor stopped me and said, "Please don't pass out those books. That subject is divisive."

His point is unscriptural. Note the first phrase of verse 23, "Whenever you come together..." It is my belief that tongues, like all the spiritual gifts, are actually rallying points for The Body of Christ. These activities prove our God is alive and doing great things. Why would we move away from such dynamic proofs?

Building Up

Inspiration gifts are designed to build up the church. Each member is a candidate for these gifts to operate through. As a close family friend is known to say before she ministers, "Let the fruit and gifts of Your Holy Spirit manifest among your people, Lord Jesus."

"He who speaks in a tongue edifies himself, but he who prophesies edifies the church," (1 Corinthians 14:4) Each time an individual prays in tongues that person is strengthened and built up. "When a tongue is manifest in a public service, the congregation is only edified when it is accompanied by an interpretation."

Tongues Operate In Two Ways

This sacred gift can function in two ways, through speaking and by singing. "Let the word of Christ dwell in you richly in all wisdom, teaching and admonishing one another in psalms and hymns and spiritual songs, singing with grace in your hearts to the Lord,"

(Colossians 3:16).

This gift can bring admonition, a word usually only understood in the sense of rebuke. However, it can also mean warning or encouragement to do right. These three activities flow through psalms, hymns, and spiritual songs.

Psalms were written for singing. They are also spoken. Hymns are forms of adoration directed toward God. Today we understand this type of action to be worship. God can receive our worship through singing or spoken affirmation of Who He is.

Spiritual songs are also called The Song of The Lord. This is a song ministered in tongues followed by an interpretation. Remember, other than for moments of corporate intercession, tongues in a public settlng must be interpreted.

The Gift of Tongues is for Everyone

I was born in Conroe, Texas. One of my friends is a successful insurance agent in that city. While visiting him he told me he admired my faithfulness to minister in tongues.

I thanked him and said, "You can flow in The Holy Spirit that way, too."

He quickly said, "The church I was saved in taught us speaking in tongues is not for everyone."

Try as I might, I got nowhere in ministering Spirit Baptism to this dear brother. His eyes were blinded by religious teaching.

Those who forbid the exercise of the gift of tongues are in a seriously bad place. Why? Read 1 Corinthians 14:39, "Therefore, brethren, desire earnestly to prophesy, and do not forbid to speak with tongues."

There was a time in The United States when tongues was even more controversial than today. I defy anyone to find a single Christian

Denomination in The United States that does not have Spirit-Filled believers in their midst who speak in tongues.

At the turn of the 20th Century less than 3/100th of the population of planet earth described themselves as "Pentecostal" or, "Spirit-Filled." Christianity is still the fastest growing faith in the world and the Pentecostal/Charismatic segment is the largest. By 2025 it is estimated that more than one billion Christians will describe themselves as "Spirit-Filled."

Writing under the unction of The Holy Spirit, Paul shared, *"I wish you all spoke with tongues,"* (1 Corinthians 14:5). If you are reading this book the odds are extremely high you believe The Bible is the literal Word and instruction of God. If The Bible says we should move in this gift, doesn't it make sense that all believers should have it in operation?

Spiritual Gifts Can Stagnate

Each of the nine charismata originally manifest by faith. They continue to operate that same way ...by faith. The more you exercise each of these spiritual gifts the stronger your faith will grow.

Gifts can atrophy like an unused muscle. During a letter to his protégé, Timothy, The Apostle Paul wrote, "Do not neglect the gift that is in you, which was given to you by prophecy with the laying on of the hands of the eldership."

I have a natural gift of singing. As a young man I traveled in Christian Music ministry, was nominated for and won awards as a singer and songwriter. I am not as consistently excellent as I was as a young man because I have not used the gift God gave me.

I am not saying a spiritual gift such as tongues "gets better" because you use it. No, I am saying you develop proficiency in using the gift. The gift does not get better, but you do develop a skill and comfort level in manifesting the gift.

Will Tongues Cease?

Dispensational cessationism is a school of Christian thought that says all supernatural activities, including healing and the nine gifts of the Holy Spirit, ceased their manifestation when the last apostle died. These scholars relish 1 Corinthians 3:8. They also misapply it.

> *"Love never fails. But whether there are prophecies, they will fail; whether there are tongues, they will cease; whether there is knowledge, it will vanish away,"* (1 Corinthians 13:8)

Instead of giving you my opinion, courtesy of The United Methodist Church, I share the interpretation of John Wesley: "Charity never faileth: but whether there be prophecies, they shall fail; whether there be tongues, they shall cease; whether there be knowledge, it shall vanish away. Love never faileth –It accompanies to, and adorns us in, eternity; it prepares us for, and constitutes, heaven.

But whether there be prophecies, they shall fail – When all things are fulfilled, and God is all in all.

Whether there be tongues, they shall cease – One language shall prevail among all the inhabitants of heaven, and the low and imperfect languages of earth be forgotten. The knowledge likewise which we now so eagerly pursue, shall then vanish away – As starlight is lost in that of the midday sun, so our present knowledge in the light of eternity."

Wesley shares above what I believe. The love of God never fails. Prophecy will end when we are in the presence of God and have no need for further insight. Tongues shall end...*at the conclusion of the church age.*

We are *in* the church age. We will remain in the church age until The Rapture of The Church.

On the day of writing these words I heard from a Christian minister in a Muslim nation. She wonders if the people of The U.S. realize how serious world conditions are.

Without the gifts of The Holy Spirit we are often oblivious as to what is going on around us. As evil increases, we don't need fewer manifestations of The Holy Spirit; we need more.

Why Will Tongues Cease?

In perfect heaven we will no longer need the Holy Spirit to guide us into the knowledge of all truth. *"However, when He, the Spirit of truth, has come, He will guide you into all truth; for He will not speak on His own authority, but whatever He hears He will speak; and He will tell you things to come,"* (John 16:13).

As I shared earlier in this chapter, one purpose of tongues is to serve as a supernatural sign to unbelievers. There will be no unbelievers in heaven.

We will no longer need our prayer language to glorify God in heaven. The language of heaven will be enough.

We will not need tongues to edify, build up, ourselves in heaven. Depression and emotional heaviness will be unknown in the eternal glory of our Perfect Lord throughout eternity.

Seven Reasons for Tongues

1. **Tongues Is Initial Evidence of Spirit Baptism.** On three occasions in The Acts The Bible describes tongues as the proof of the believers having received the fullness of The Spirit. On The Day of Pentecost: "And they were all filled with the Holy Spirit and began to speak with other tongues, as the Spirit gave them utterance, (Acts 2:4); **Ten Years Later:** *While Peter was still speaking these words, the Holy Spirit fell upon all those who heard the word. And those of the circumcision who believed were astonished, as many as came with Peter, because the gift of the Holy Spirit had been poured out on the Gentiles also. For they heard them speak with tongues and magnify God. Then Peter answered, "Can anyone forbid water, that these should not be baptized who have received the Holy Spirit just as we have?" And he commanded them to be baptized in the name of the Lord. Then they asked him to stay a few days,"* (Acts 10:44-48); **20 Years After Pentecost:** *When they heard this, they were baptized in the name of the Lord Jesus. And when Paul had laid hands on them, the Holy Spirit came upon them, and they spoke with tongues and prophesied,* (Acts 19:5-6).

2. **Tongues Is The Prayer Language of The Holy Spirit.** When we pray in tongues our mental process is disengaged. Our human spirit...the real us...is able to talk to God without earthly interference. *"For he who speaks in a tongue does not speak to men but to God, for no one understands him; however, in the spirit he speaks mysteries,"* (1 Corinthians 14:2).

3. **Tongues Magnify God.** Tongues make the voice of God louder to the inner man, and make Him larger in our sanctified imagination where all things become possible. *"For they heard them speak with tongues and magnify God,"* (Acts 10:46).

4. **Tongues Edify.** Spiritual strength comes to those who pray in tongues. *"He who speaks in a tongue edifies himself, but he who prophesies edifies the church,"* (1 Corinthians 14:4).

5. **Tongues Frees Joy To Flow Through Singing.** "What is the conclusion then? I will pray with the spirit, and I will also pray with the understanding. I will sing with the spirit, and I will also sing with the understanding," (1 Corinthians 14:15).

6. **Tongues Empowers Intercessory Prayer.** One of the most powerful ministries of the local church is intercessory prayer. When England was about to lose her entire army to Hitler on the French Coast at Dunkirk, Prime Minister Winston Churchill called for a national day of prayer and fasting. The British Army was saved and Nazi Germany was eventually defeated. *"Likewise the Spirit also helps in our weaknesses. For we do not know what we should pray for as we ought, but the Spirit Himself makes intercession for us with groanings which cannot be uttered,"* (Romans 5:26).

7. **Tongues Releases Spiritual Refreshing.** *"For with stammering lips and another tongue He will speak to this people, To whom He said, 'This is the rest with which you may cause the weary to rest,' And, 'This is the refreshing...'"* (Isaiah 28:11-12).

Charge your spirit by praying in tongues.

We should not pray in tongues less.

We should pray in tongues more.

Chapter Fifteen

The Gift of the Interpretation of Tongues

The ninth of the Charismatic Gifts and the third of The Gifts of Inspiration is the Gift of The Interpretation of Tongues.

This gift is dependent upon the gift of tongues, someone publicly speaking (ministering) a message in a language they do not know.

The Gift of The Interpretation of Tongues is necessary to make the message in tongues understood to the Body of Christ. The interpreter hears a language he or she does not speak, but gives the interpretation in a natural language under the anointing of The Holy Spirit.

A Companion Gift to be Sought

Simply stated, if you minister in tongues you should ask God to manifest through you the gift of interpretation. This is the Biblical pattern, *"Therefore let him who speaks in a tongue pray that he may interpret,"* (1 Corinthians 14:13).

Again, apart from a time when the entire congregation prays in agreement in tongues, a public tongue with no interpretation is a sign of disorder.

A Personally Held Belief

It is my belief that all pastors should move in the interpretation of tongues. Why? For the sake of governmental order.

I grew up among wonderful people who were actually frightened by the manifestation of the gifts of the Holy Spirit among them. During the term of one pastor a tongue would go forth and a "holy hush" would follow with the pastor then saying, "Someone needs to obey God."

Every Spirit-filled believer is capable of moving in the gift of the interpretation of the tongues. However, for the sake of order, I believe it is an absolute must that the pastor, or a designated staff member, be the interpreter for the body.

Years ago I served as an associate pastor of a booming Word of Faith Church in Houston, Texas. The pastor had great confidence, publicly expressed, in my flow as an interpreter. He even went so far as to announce during my few absences, "Our interpreter is not with us today. If you have something stirring, please hold it until Pastor Malcolm returns."

He valued the manifestation gifts, but had no comfort level in moving in anything other than preaching and the gifts of healing. As much as I still value his appreciation of the gift of God within me, I wish he would have overcome his sense of hesitation.

Tips For Interpreters

1. **The Gift Of Interpretation Is Designed To Edify The Church.** When the gift of interpretation of tongues is linked with its companion gift, the gift of tongues, it equals prophecy. As we have noted several times from 1 Corinthians 14:4, this then edifies the church. If you sense what you are about to share is not edifying, stop.

2. **Tongues Plus Interpretation Allows People To Observe A Miracle.** This activity is no "light" thing. Tongues alone can confuse the unbeliever, but clarity comes when the interpretation is linked. My Uncle Doug is in heaven now. He was a member of the cessation church my grandparents raised him in. He was completely opposed to tongues due to seeing the gift mishandled. Upon hearing a tongue with an accompanying interpretation, his attitude changed. During that church service he realized we were as much a part of Orthodox Christianity as he and his home congregation.

3. **The Interpretation of Tongues Is Not a Translation.** One Sunday morning a staff member informed me she had a tongue to minister. She spoke forth the tongue and I gave the interpretation. Afterward, a young man approached me, "Pastor, she spoke less words than you did." My answer was easy. It was an interpretation, not a translation. A translation is more word for word. The phrasing of an interpretation will be different. Dr. Sumrall said, "A translation is an exact rendering from one language to another in precise grammatical terms; an interpretation reveals what God wants us to know. This explains why at times a message in tongues might be long while the interpretation is short."

4. **Human Personality Is Often Part of The Interpretation of Tongues.** On a trip to Mainland China, an interpreter seemed to be preaching her own sermon. As she continued I realized she was interpreting my message, not translating it. How did I know what she was doing was acceptable? The power of The Gospel was unleashed. People were blessed, lives were changed. Dr. Jeff Thompson shared a powerful truth, "Just like water can assume the taste of the water pipe, so can the interpretation convey the taste of the conduit it flows through."

5. **The Interpretation of Tongues Is Not A Product of The Human Mind.** Even though personality will shine through, the mind is not involved because the interpreter does not speak the language. This is not an activity where the interpreter is given time to go away and "think up" an interpretation. A smooth flow is one proof of the purity of the product.

6. **The Tongue May Cause The Interpreter To Visualize What Is To Be Spoken Forth.** This has happened with me on countless occasions. The tongue "kick starts" my faith and I see what God wants said.

7. **The Interpretation of Tongues Always Requires Faith.** In almost every case I have only been given a few words at a time. On several occasions I have been exposed to the ministry of The Rev. Mr. Mark Hankins. After ministering together in a service

at his brother's church, Pastor Bob, at West Columbia Assembly of God, I asked Mark about what I had observed. His wife, The Rev. Trina Hankins, spoke in tongues over one minister for several minutes. Mark gave an even longer interpretation. I wondered if the "whole thing" had been spelled out for him before he began to speak. To my blessing, he said, "No, it literally came forth a few words at a time. As I moved in faith and spoke what had been revealed, more words came."

A Country Lady

God knows what He is doing. He can even use tongues to share a message with someone away from relationship with him.

I preached in Porter, Texas at age nineteen. In those days it was an outpost rather than the suburb of Metropolitan Houston it is today.

Testimonies were customary in those days. I asked if God had done anything unusual for anyone during the meeting.

A lady stood and told of having outpatient surgery that morning. As she recovered her physician came into her room and greeted her in a language she did not understand. He said, "Come on! I know you speak Greek!"

"No," she said, "I do not speak a word of Greek. For that matter, my English is not too good."

The physician had a shocked expression upon his face. "You must speak Greek. You called me by my Greek nickname and said God was calling me back to Him. You even stated how much I loved serving as an altar boy in The Greek Orthodox Church."

Completely astonished, the lady recounted how the doctor began to pray quietly there in the recovery room. The physician told her he was repentant and returning to God. Clearly this was a manifestation of tongues, accompanied by what would appear to be a natural interpretation.

Operating In The Interpretation of Tongues

In most churches the gifts of The Holy Spirit do not manifest because they are not desired. In others they cease to function because of unscriptural practices. One of my relatives attends a church I had known to be active in the gifts of the Holy Spirit. Misuse has caused that portion of God's light to be extinguished.

I know this is repetitive, but I am sharing it again for a reason. Ecstatic outbursts of tongues with no interpretation has brought confusion to many congregations. Rather than train the person desiring to be used of God in this arena the practice was ended all together.

Paul tells us, *"I thank my God I speak with tongues more than you all; yet in the church I would rather speak five words with my understanding, that I may teach others also, than ten thousand words in a tongue,"* (1 Corinthians 14:18-19).

Limited Manifestation

Another appeal for order is given in outline form.

"How is it then, brethren? Whenever you come together, each of you has a psalm, has a teaching, has a tongue, has a revelation, has an interpretation. Let all things be done for edification. If anyone speaks in a tongue, let there be two or at the most three, each in turn, and let one interpret,"

(1 Corinthians 14:26-27)

The manifestation of three segments of tongues is the maximum for a church service. An interpretation should follow each communication in tongues. Why? *"For God is not the author of confusion but of peace, as in all the churches of the saints,"* (1 Corinthians 14:33).

Please note that this does not mean only three manifestations of tongues in a service. It means three segments. There may be tongues, interpretation and more tongues followed by still more interpretation. Do not be legalistic in your thinking. Give some room for reason to work in this instance.

When you speak to your child on a subject you may not say everything in one paragraph. Your communication, especially an instructive one, often contains more than one statement. The same is so with your Heavenly Father's communication to you.

Believers Meetings

I believe this restriction to three segments of tongues does not apply in Believers Meetings. The point of the limitation is order and makes perfect sense when unbelievers may be present. When spiritually sincere people come together for the purpose of creating a climate in which spiritual gifts may operate such a limit is not necessary.

During this season in my life I am enjoying conducting "The School of The Holy Spirit." These are believers meetings held around the country to encourage believers to stir their faith for manifestations of The Holy Spirit. The climate is one of mature faith and receptivity for manifestations, much different than most church services.

The Elim Model

While I do not share their belief that The British Empire is actually "British Israel", I do enjoy fellowship with Elim Churches. Their services are rich with the presence of God and permeated with expectation of Divine involvement in human affairs.

Even with these exciting things, above all, I respect Elim's insistence upon Divine order. At an Elim Conference the moderator of the meetings will announce the interpreter for the meetings.

When an individual has a tongue he moves to the front of the building and secures the attention of the moderator. If the moderator believes the time to be right the person is allowed to give the tongue and the interpreter shares the message.

While there may be different persons ministering in tongues, there is only one interpreter. I am not trying to be legalistic, but note the command of scripture, *"If anyone speaks in a tongue, let there be two or at the most three, each in turn, and let one interpret,"* (1 Corinthians 14:27).

A Flatly Stated Point of Order

No manifestation of tongues is the rule when there is no interpreter present. *"But if there is no interpreter, let him keep silent in church, and let him speak to himself and to God,"* (1 Corinthians 14:28).

Take a moment to look with me at an overlooked point here. The command is to let him speak to himself *"...and to God."*

If there is no interpreter present demonstrate your respect for protocol by quietly releasing the tongue into the atmosphere as something directed *"to God."*

Statements I Cannot Stand

The Bible is clear that we are to have control over the situation when we are operating in spiritual gifts. Yet, I grew up hearing outbursts in tongues followed by explanations such as:

1. "That wasn't me. That was God."

2. "I couldn't' help myself."

3. "God made me do it."

4. "Don't judge me."

All four statements are incorrect. Consider these verses as instruction: *"Let two or three prophets speak, and let the others judge. But if anything is revealed to another who sits by, let the first keep silent. For you can all prophesy one by one, that all may learn and all may be encouraged. And the spirits of the prophets are subject to the prophets,"* (1 Corinthians 14:29-32).

Again, tongues plus interpretation equals prophecy. I see five conclusions about this prophetic ministry contained in verses 29-32.

1. More than one person can speak.

2. Prophecy is to be judged as to whether or not it is of God.

3. Prophetic ministers must be in submission to each other.

4. Prophetic ministers must speak in an orderly manner.

5. You are in control of what you say and do.

God is always willing to do His part. We must be willing to do ours.

If you are a Spirit-filled believer, you qualify to be used in the gifts of The Holy Spirit.

Decide to make yourself available to be used of God.

You will not regret the decision.

CPSIA information can be obtained
at www.ICGtesting.com
Printed in the USA
FSHW022356011218
53967FS